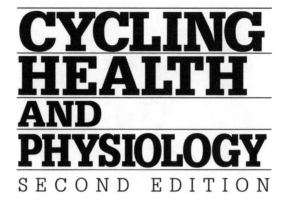

CYCLING
HEALTH
AND
PHYSIOLOGY

SECOND EDITION

SECOND EDITION

ED BURKE, PH.D.

CYCLING HEALTH AND PHYSIOLOGY

USING SPORTS SCIENCE TO IMPROVE YOUR RIDING AND RACING

VITESSE PRESS • COLLEGE PARK, MARYLAND

Cycling Health and Physiology

Published by Vitesse Press
4431 Lehigh Road, #288
College Park, MD 20740

Library of Congress Cataloging-in-Publication Data

Burke, Ed., 1949-
    Cycling health and physiology : using sports science to improve
    your riding and racing / Edmund R. Burke. -- [2nd ed.]
        p.   cm.
    Includes index.
    ISBN 0-941950-34-4
    1. Cycling -- Physiological aspects. 2. Cycling -- Health aspects.
    I. Title.
    RC1220.C8B87 1998
     613.7'11--DC21   97-42785
                                         CIP

Cover and text design by James Brisson
Drawings by Jane Swanson

Manufactured in the United States of America

10 9 8 7 6 5 4 3 2 1

Distributed in the United States by Alan C. Hood, Inc. (717-267-0867)

For sales inquiries and special prices for bulk quantities, contact Vitesse Press at 301-772-5915 or write to the address above.

CONTENTS

HEALTH

ABOUT THE AUTHOR

Ed Burke, Ph.D. is a former competitive rider who turned his interest in cycling into his major field of study. Currently a professor and the director of the Exercise Science Program at the University of Colorado at Colorado Springs, he conducts research in cycling performance, sports nutrition, fitness and adaptations to training. Prior to his current position, he was Director of Product Development at Spenco Medical Corporation where he coordinated outside research and the development on sports medicine products.

Burke holds a doctorate in Exercise Physiology from Ohio State University and was a N.I.H. postdoctoral fellow in the Department of Internal Medicine at the University of Iowa Hospitals.

Dr. Burke is also a Fellow of the American College of Sports Medicine and a Certified Strength and Conditioning Specialist (CSCS) with the National Strength and Conditioning Association. He has served as vice-president for the National Strength and Conditioning Association. In addition, he serves as one of the national spokespersons for the POLAR Precision Fitness Institute.

He was Coordinator of Sports Sciences for the U. S. Cycling

Team leading up to the Olympic Games in 1996 and a staff member for the 1980 and 1984 Olympic Cycling Teams. Dr. Burke directed the Center for Science and Technology for the U. S. Cycling Team, Colorado Springs, CO from 1982 to 1987.

Over the past decade, Burke has become one on the leading experts on sports medicine. He has taught exercise physiology and fitness classes and continues to lecture both nationally and internationally on various topics in physiology, nutrition, health and fitness matters. He has written or co-authored over 25 peer reviewed scientific articles for various scientific journals. In addition, he writes columns for *Winning Magazine, Mountain Biker, Muscular Development, Nutritional Science News* and *NORBA News* and answers fitness questions for a column in *Bicycling Magazine.*

Ed Burke has written or edited fourteen books including *Cycling Stronger, Fitness Cycling* (co-authored with Chris Carmichael), *Serious Cycling, Getting In Shape: Programs for Men and Women* (with Bob Anderson, author of *Stretching* and Bill Pearl, author of *Getting Stronger), Training Nutrition* (co-authored with Jackie Berning, Ph.D., R.D.), and *The Complete Home Fitness Handbook.*

Dr. Burke is currently a consultant to several companies in the areas of cycling technology, fitness equipment design, nutritional products and fitness programs and sits on the boards of directors of two corporations. He has also developed athletic drinks and nutritionals, sports drinking systems and other sports equipment.

He enjoys riding his road and mountain bikes, cross-country skiing and hiking in the mountains of Colorado and has completed the Pikes Peak marathon, trekked into Everest Base camp, and completed the Leadville 100 mile mountain bike race. He enjoys reading books on business, health and nutrition.

PREFACE

"Those who are enamored of practice without
science are like a pilot who goes into a ship
without a rudder or compass and never
has any certainty of where he is going."
— LEONARDO DA VINCI

Successful cyclists are scientists in the truest sense of the
word. They are constantly evaluating and re-evaluating. They
ask questions of other athletes, coaches, and experts. They are
experimenters, and in experimenting they try new ideas such
as anaerobic threshold training, plyometrics, or ergometer
work.

Like any scientist, the successful cyclist is curious and at
times may even be confused. He is able to recognize the
source of his confusion, and often this confusion keeps him
in search of the truth. He is constantly looking for new approaches and improved techniques. He is always searching for
the proper application of science to sport.

That's where this book comes in. I hope it will provide the
foundation in physiology — Leonardo's "rudder" — that will
enable you to construct a sound training plan. Understanding
the underlying physical responses can help you fine tune your
fitness program. Concepts of human energy, for example, can
be used in understanding how to prevent or delay fatigue, how
nutrition contributes to performance, how to effectively control body weight, and how the body's temperature is controlled
and maintained.

I hope that after reading this book you'll feel more comfortable applying science to your training program. Not every
cyclist can be a winner, but with hard work and intelligent
training, you can achieve the best that is within you.

ACKNOWLEDGMENTS

I am indebted to many people for the ideas and information in this book, including cycling and scientific researchers throughout the world; Eddie Borysewicz and all the coaches and cyclists who helped me better understand the sport; Marilee Attley for her help in editing and rewriting much of the text; and all the publishers and editors over the last 20 years who have helped me share information with the cyclists of the world.

And finally, I owe the greatest debt to my wife Kathleen. She has unselfishly provided the understanding, the encouragement, and the patience that has allowed me to devote an inordinate amount of time to cycling and writing.

PHYSIOLOGY

1 / Heart and other muscles

Have you ever wondered what secret certain riders possess that enables them to win race after race while the rest of us simply fill in the pack? Did they break through the pain barrier during winter training in Florida while we cursed the snow? Do they know some mechanical secret that we have yet to discover? Or do they simply have more of that mysterious quality known as talent?

Research indicates that winning cyclists may indeed possess certain physical qualities that give them an advantage over the rest of the field. One of the most important of these qualities is excellent aerobic power.

Train for aerobic power

Aerobic power (also called max VO_2) is the maximum amount of oxygen that a person can use during exhaustive work. The greater the rate of oxygen delivered to the muscles, the greater the rate of work or speed that can be maintained. Aerobic power is generally considered the best single indicator of cardiorespiratory capacity (the functioning ability of the heart and lungs). Highly trained male cyclists have max VO_2 levels (indicated in milliliters of oxygen consumed per kilogram of body weight per minute) of between 70 and 80 ml/kg, while lesser trained or female riders have values of 50-60 ml/kg.

A study of racers in various categories reveals that racers in the higher categories generally have higher aerobic power. Clearly, aerobic power and racing performance are related.

What determines aerobic power? Heredity plays a large part. Some people are blessed with higher maximal cardiac output (the amount of blood the heart can pump per minute). The difference between a person with great cardiac output and one with a more nominal value appears to be stroke volume — the amount of blood that can be pumped with each heart beat. This suggests that some people may have larger-than-normal hearts. The idea isn't so startling when we consider the variation in other anatomical features. If tall individuals have a natural advantage in basketball, why shouldn't people with large hearts dominate endurance sports like cycling?

Does this mean that unless your aerobic power tests out above 70 ml/kg you can't hope to reach the top in cycling? Maybe, but probably not. For one thing, the range of aerobic power among cyclists is very large. We've tested Category III riders with max VO_2 above 65 ml/kg and Category I riders as low as 60 ml/kg. This certainly proves that aerobic power is not the sole determinant of success.

And training makes a difference. You can substantially increase your aerobic power with the proper training methods, but there does appear to be a limit to the amount of improvement you can achieve. An active individual who changes his training may increase his max VO_2 by up to 25%, but no matter how many miles he covers or how many interval workouts he does, he won't be able to double the original value.

Riding more miles does not necessarily increase aerobic power. In fact, it appears that aerobic power increases most with relatively modest amounts of training. (See graph.) In other words, the person who rides 200 miles a week will not develop twice the aerobic power of one who only rides 100 miles. The type of training is as important as the amount.

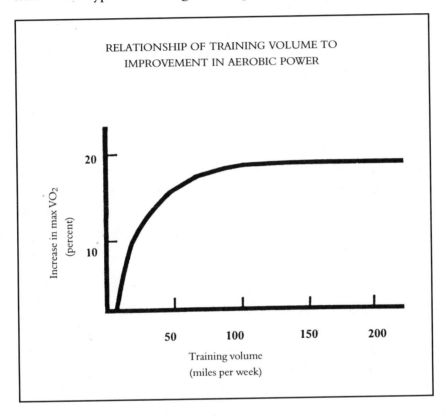

RELATIONSHIP OF TRAINING VOLUME TO
IMPROVEMENT IN AEROBIC POWER

Riding more miles can help increase your maximal oxygen uptake, and hence your ability to do exhaustive work. But there is a limit. Improvement comes with relatively modest amounts of training, then tapers off.

As training progresses, however, a rider may see a marked improvement in performance even though his aerobic power does not change. For example, it often happens that a cyclist performs at the same level as his more athletically gifted competitors by by increasing the distance or intensity of his training. This suggests that within certain limits, a highly motivated cyclist with less than super talent may perform quite well. This improved performance is probably caused by changes in the muscle tissue.

How muscles work

Muscles produce tension for work by shortening (contracting). When muscles contract they use large amounts of energy. However, the amount of energy stored in the muscles is very limited, so working muscles must depend on blood flow for delivery of adequate amounts of fuel.

All cells depend on a chemical compound, adenosine triphosphate (ATP), for their immediate energy source. Energy from food must first be transformed by the cells into ATP before it can be used. When ATP is broken down by chemical action, energy is released. This breakdown is achieved two ways: with oxygen (aerobic metabolism), and without oxygen (anaerobic metabolism).

During aerobic metabolism, oxygen is used to manufacture ATP from fats, carbohydrates, and, to a lesser extent, proteins. The by-products of aerobic metabolism are carbon dioxide and water. Carbon dioxide is easily diffused into the bloodstream and then carried to the lungs to be exhaled, while water is used by the cell itself. Since it produces no fatiguing by-products, aerobic metabolism can be carried on for long periods of time and can produce large amounts of energy.

There are two forms of anaerobic metabolism: the ATP-PC system and the lactic acid system. The ATP-PC system gets its name from phosphocreatine, a substance in the cell that is used to synthesize ATP. Energy derived from the ATP-PC system is very limited, fueling activities that last no longer than 10-15 seconds. Though the energy it provides is minimal, ATP-PC energy can be produced rapidly. ATP-PC systems come into play when explosive power is needed, such as in the finish of a road race or match sprint.

In the lactic acid energy system (also known as anaerobic glycolysis) carbohydrates are broken down to ATP without the aid of oxygen. The lack of oxygen means that the carbohydrates can only be partially broken down, leaving lactic acid as a by-product. When lactic acid reaches a high enough level, it prevents muscle contraction. So lactic acid metabolism can only be carried out for short periods of time. Exercise performed at maximum levels for one to three minutes depends heavily on the lactic acid system.

Muscle fibers, the inside story

Until the early '70s, it was difficult to study exactly what happens inside muscles during exercise, but the technique of muscle biopsy has changed all that. With muscle biopsy we can safely gain valuable information about an individual's physiological make-up.

To perform a muscle biopsy, researchers use a biopsy needle that is three to five millimeters in diameter (about the size of a pencil). The subject is given a local anaesthetic, and then a half-inch incision is made into the muscle and the needle inserted. Since muscle has no pain receptors, the insertion doesn't hurt. The sensation is usually described only as "weird."

A sample of 20-40 milligrams of muscle tissue is extracted, enough for several biochemical tests, including fiber typing.

All muscle fibers contract to their greatest possible tension when stimulated. However, fibers differ in their rate of contraction. Certain muscle fibers can contract repeatedly without much fatigue. This type is known as red fiber because of its high content of myoglobin (an oxygen-storing protein that gives the tissue a red color). It has a high aerobic capacity, which means it can produce energy at a steady rate for a long time when enough oxygen is available. Red fiber develops peak tension slowly, about 0.1 seconds after stimulation. Because of this, red fiber is also called slow-twitch (ST) fiber.

The other major fiber type has less myoglobin, which makes it look whiter. This fiber develops tension rather fast (0.02-0.03 seconds) but fatigues easily. The traditional name for this fiber is white fiber, but it's better known as fast-twitch (FT) fiber.

ST and FT fibers also have different capacities for breaking down glycogen and accumulating lactic acid. That is, they have different anaerobic capacities. In this regard fast-twitch fibers are superior. They can perform short-term, very intense work without abundant oxygen.

That isn't the whole story, though. ST and FT fibers contain a whole spectrum of aerobic and anaerobic potential. One person's FT fibers may have a greater aerobic capacity than another person's, but within an individual, the ST fibers will usually have a higher aerobic capacity than the FT fibers. The FT fibers, on the other hand, will have a higher anaerobic capacity.

Training can enhance the aerobic or anaerobic capacity of either type of muscle fiber. So a cyclist who has trained for long races may have a higher aerobic capacity in the FT fibers of his legs than in the ST fibers of his arms. What training can't change is an individual's actual ratio of ST to FT fibers. Heredity determines that.

Typically, muscle fiber in the average person is composed of 40-50% ST and 50-60% FT, though these ratios may vary from person to person. However, within an individual, only small variations appear to exist from one muscle to another. The sole exception is the soleus muscle (a calf muscle), which is mainly composed of ST fibers.

What's "ideal" fiber makeup?

Do cyclists need a specific fiber ratio and do certain events favor cyclists who are more ST or FT?

For an event like match sprinting, the answer seems clear. A sprinter needs a high percentage of FT fibers because his event is primarily anaerobic. Weight training and sprint workouts can develop the strength and anaerobic capacity of these fibers even further.

It's more difficult to determine an ideal fiber make-up for middle- and long-distance road racers. However, a recent study by Danish researchers gives some clues. The researchers tested 44 subjects, including 19 professional road racers, 3 pro track racers, 6 amateur competitors, and 4 former pro road racers who hadn't trained for 20 years. Six physical education students and six completely untrained subjects were studied as controls.

The slow-twitch percentage for the pro road cyclists ranged from 55-85% with the mean value being 71%, while the untrained subjects had values of 47-70%. These findings support the idea that ST fibers are best suited for endurance activities. It should be noted, however, that FT fibers are also very important for elite road racers because periodic sprints and accelerations occur frequently during races. In this regard it was found that the two elite road racers with the lowest percentage of ST fibers, 55% and 56%, respectively, were among the four best sprinters, while the racer with the highest percentage of ST fibers (85%) was among those most successful in the mountains.

The size of the fibers themselves was also interesting. In the untrained subjects, the ST fibers were typically smaller than the FT, while in the elite cyclists, the two fiber types were essentially the same size. In other words, the elite cyclists not only had a higher percentage of ST, but the fibers themselves were larger. This indicates that while you can't change your fiber makeup, proper training can increase the size of the fibers and improve their function.

Does this mean that only riders with 75% well-developed ST fibers will do well in long road races? No. Because so much energy output goes into overcoming wind resistance, a cyclist with mediocre aerobic capacity and a low percentage of ST fibers can, by drafting, keep pace with the best riders in the peloton. This is especially true on flat courses.

A major question is why one rider can greatly improve endurance while others with the same fiber ratio cannot. The answer is partly related to training methods, but there is another consideration. FT fibers can be subdivided into two types. One type will improve its aerobic capacity relatively easily while the other appears to resist endurance training. Champion cyclists probably have more of the first type. One purpose of training is to develop the aerobic and anaerobic capacities of muscles. It makes sense to plan workouts so they will consolidate strengths and eliminate weaknesses. A cyclist who is predominantly FT will already have the edge in anaerobic capacity. He needs to develop his aerobic ability. The reverse holds true for a cyclist who is mostly ST.

How can you tell what your muscle fiber composition is? A biopsy is the only precise way to find out, but it's likely you already know, in a general way, what your ratio is. If you've had a variety of racing experiences and kept a training diary, you probably have a pretty good idea where your strengths and weaknesses lie. You know if you have good speed, good endurance, or a certain mixture of these qualities. Almost every serious cyclist already knows whether to do more endurance work to develop aerobic ability or more speedwork to develop anaerobic ability. It isn't necessary to have a biopsy to figure it out.

Warm-up gets muscles working

One thing that helps muscles function at their best is a warm-up before hard training or racing. Warming up is beneficial for several reasons:

— Muscle temperature increases. A warmed muscle contracts more forcefully and relaxes more quickly than a cold one. This enhances both speed and strength and reduces the likelihood of muscles being overstretched and injured.

— Blood temperature increases. As it travels through the muscle, the temperature of the blood increases. As blood warms, the amount of oxygen it can hold is reduced. The blood gives up the oxygen to the muscles, so a slightly greater volume of oxygen is made available to the working muscles, enhancing endurance and performance.

— Range of motion improves. The range of motion around joints increases, especially if flexibility exercises are part of the warm-up.

— Hormone production increases. More of the hormones responsible for regulating energy production are produced. They, in turn, begin making more carbohydrates and fatty acids available for energy production.

— Metabolism, the body's ability to process energy, improves. For every one-degree rise in body temperature, metabolism within a muscle cell increases approximately 13%. As a result the exchange of oxygen from blood to muscle is improved.

How long should your warm-up be? It's really a matter of individual preference. A gradual warm-up of 10-15 minutes seems to result in better performance than a quick 5-minute one. How can you tell when you've warmed-up long enough? In general, when you break into a sweat, you've raised your internal temperature to the desired level.

The positive effects of a warm-up may last as long as 45 minutes, but the closer your warm-up is to the start of an event, the more it will benefit performance. Your warm-up should begin to taper off 10-15 minutes before the race and end with 5-10 minutes remaining. This will allow recovery from any slight fatigue.

A warm-up on the bike usually consists of riding a few miles and adding a few short jumps to be sure that all the muscles are warmed up. This is known as a related warm-up, because it incorporates the specific skills of cycling. In unrelated warm-ups the movements performed, such as calisthenics or flexibility exercises, are different from the actual skills used in the race.

Which type of warm-up is best? If jumping right into some aspect of competition would result in injury, then an unrelated warm-up is preferable. For instance, cyclocross and mountain bike riding demand great flexibility. If a rider were to dismount quickly and jump an obstacle before doing stretching exercises for his legs, back, and hips, he might strain a muscle. For the same reason, track cyclists usually begin their warm-up with some sort of unrelated exercise.

Whatever warm-up you choose, it should be intense enough to increase body temperature but not so intense as to make you tired. Research has shown that an adequate warm-up prevents muscle strains, tears, and soreness that would probably occur if the athlete went into full performance without it.

Cool-down aids recovery

The cool-down is not as widely practiced as the warm-up, but it is no less important. A cool-down helps your circulatory and metabolic systems return gradually to resting levels. There are several benefits of a cool-down.

— Lactic acid dissipates. Mild exercise speeds up the removal of lactic acid from the blood and muscles, which is thought to aid recovery.
— Blood flow returns to normal. During exercise, the blood vessels that bring oxygen and nutrients to your working muscles are wide open. A cool-down helps the blood return to the heart and allows blood vessels to return to normal size.
— Blood doesn't pool. If you stop exercising quickly, blood accumulates in the wide-open blood vessels, and especially in the legs. Not enough blood returns to the heart, so the heart beats faster in an attempt to increase blood flow. Dizziness or light-headedness can result.

A cool-down usually consists of easy cycling. After a hard effort, downshift and let your legs relax. Keep pedaling easily until your heart rate returns to below 120 beats per minute. After you get off the bike, do some non-bouncing stretches to help prevent muscle tightness and to increase flexibility. Pay particular attention to the muscle groups that are central to cycling — hamstring, quadriceps, and lower back.

2 / Aerobic and anaerobic systems

In 1996, Chris Boardman rode over 56 kilometers per hour to a world record for the distance ridden in one hour. It was a record that was destined to be broken on a regular basis over the past decade, due to continued advances in equipment technology and training techniques. Boardman accomplished the feat by applying science to training and maintaining a pace at or just below his anaerobic threshold.

Your key to endurance

Your anaerobic threshold (AT) is the workload intensity at which lactic acid begins to accumulate in your cells, even during work that requires less than maximal oxygen uptake (max VO_2). It is usually stated as a percentage of your max VO_2, but can also be indicated by a specific heart rate or by speed (mph).

Your anaerobic threshold is critical in determining your potential to perform prolonged physical exercise. As an example, suppose that three cyclists have respective max VO_2 values of 75, 70, and 70 ml/kg/min. Cyclists 1 and 3 have high anaerobic thresholds of 60 and 55 ml/kg/min, while cyclist 2 has been laying off the training and has an anaerobic threshold of only 45. In a long race, cyclist 1 can maintain a pace requiring

60 ml/kg/min and build up very little lactic acid, whereas cyclists 2 and 3, in order to keep up, must work more anaerobically and therefore produce more lactic acid. Cyclist 1 should be able to ride longer at a faster pace.

Another example: The graph shows the breathing response of two cyclists to a max VO_2 test on a bicycle ergometer. Cyclist A has a lower max VO_2 and anaerobic threshold than cyclist B. It can be seen that the breakaway point of ventilation (the point at which the breathing rate suddenly increases) is at a higher workload in cyclist B. For example, at a workload

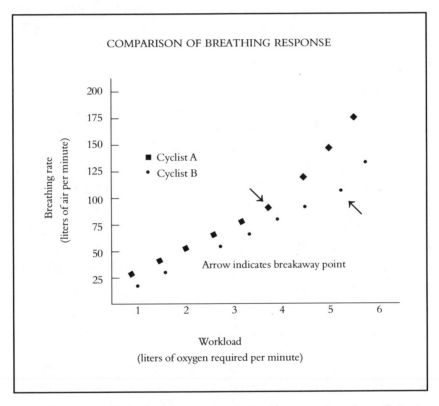

One indicator of anaerobic threshold is the breakaway point of ventilation, the point at which breathing suddenly increases. With a higher VO_2 max (maximum breathing rate) and anaerobic threshold (breakaway point), cyclist B can handle a greater workload more efficiently than A.

requiring 4.5 liters of oxygen per minute, cyclist A's ventilation would be approximately 25 liters per minute faster than cyclist B's. So cyclist A has to work harder simply to breathe, a fact that will eventually take its toll.

A cyclist with a low anaerobic threshold is also at a disadvantage when it comes to using fats as an energy source because lactic acid in the blood interferes with the release of fatty acid, which is essential for metabolizing fat for energy.

AT may be a more reliable indicator of performance than max VO_2, and studies show AT responds well to training. While you may be able to increase your max VO_2 by up to 25% with proper training, researchers have found that AT may be increased as much as 44%.

Researchers disagree somewhat on the exact definition of AT and how to determine it. Some believe it is signaled by a rapid increase in the lactic acid concentration in the blood or that it occurs when a certain level of lactic acid — usually 4 millimoles per liter — is exceeded. Others contend that an abrupt change in breathing rate signals the onset of AT, while still others believe that AT occurs when the increase in heart rate is proportionally less than the increase in speed.

All of these methods depend on locating a change in some physiological variable as speed increases, which can be a problem because changes in lactic acid concentration and breathing rates are not always clear cut.

Finding your anaerobic threshold

So how do you know when you've reached your anaerobic threshold? There are several subjective indications. During steady-pace riding, you reach a point where your breathing suddenly increases. (This breakaway point in ventilation is a result of the buffering action of lactic acid in the blood that generates excess carbon dioxide. You begin to hyperventilate in order to blow off the excess carbon dioxide.) You may also notice a burning sensation in your muscles, or find that you cannot hold the pace.

A more exact way to determine AT is through blood testing. In this procedure, heart rate is monitored while the workload is steadily increased. To obtain blood samples, your finger is pricked at regular intervals, usually every three minutes. Your heart rate is monitored throughout the test. The blood is then run through an analyzer to measure the lactic acid content. The point at which lactic acid exceeds 4 millimoles per liter is your anaerobic threshold. You then use the corresponding heart rate as a guide in your training. This procedure has some disadvantages. It's costly and you need access to high-tech equipment and skilled technicians, all of which make it difficult to repeat often during the season.

Using the Test Conconi

Another method of finding AT is to use the Test Conconi. Developed by Italian physiologist Francesco Conconi and used extensively by Moser in his training for the hour record, this non-invasive procedure determines AT by monitoring heart rate as effort is steadily increased.

The Test Conconi can be done on a track or indoors on a wind trainer. You need a reliable heart rate monitor, a stopwatch, and an assistant to record speed and heart rate as the test progresses. It is also helpful to have a cycling computer to help you accurately measure your speed. Warm up for 15-30 minutes before the test begins. When your speed evens out at 10 mph, start the stopwatch. Concentrate on maintaining a steady pace. At the end of each minute you will increase your speed by 1 mph. Your assistant should record your heart rate at the end of each one-minute period and should tell you when to increase your speed.

Continue increasing your speed at one-minute intervals until you feel the effects of lactic acid accumulation, such as a burning sensation in your legs, or until you become tired. (You don't have to keep pedaling to the point of exhaustion.) Be sure to cool down afterward with several minutes of easy pedaling.

To determine your AT, you'll need a piece of graph paper on which to plot your heart rate versus speed squared. (Speed is squared because air resistance, and therefore work and power, is proportional to the square of the velocity.) The points should form a straight line at the slower speeds but as speed increases, the line should form a knee or deflection. The point at which this deflection occurs indicates your anaerobic threshold. (See graph.)

The advantage of the Test Conconi is that it's inexpensive and can be done every two to four weeks to monitor your training progress. (It should be noted, however, that researchers disagree on the validity and accuracy of the Test Conconi. More research is being done to determine other ways of finding AT.)

Once you have determined your AT, how do you go about using it in your training? Conconi suggests that to improve your threshold, you should do a certain portion of your training at a level within 10% of your AT. You will have to experiment to see just how much training you need or can tolerate at this intensity.

Lactic acid hurts

We've all felt the severe leg pain that comes at the end of a hard jam or fast climb. This pain is caused, in part, by lactic acid build-up in the muscle cells.

Lactic acid is the end product of anaerobic metabolism, which occurs when there is not enough oxygen to produce the

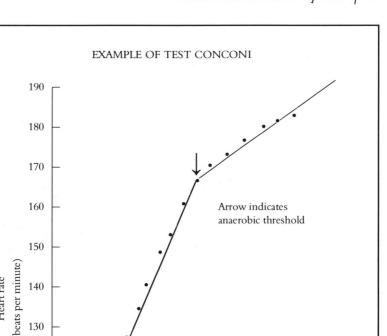

EXAMPLE OF TEST CONCONI

Arrow indicates
anaerobic threshold

Heart rate
(beats per minute)

Speed
(miles per hour, squared)

You can find your anaerobic threshold by monitoring your heart rate as you
gradually increase your speed. At the threshold your heart rate no longer
increases in the same proportion as your speed. The graph is plotted on a
speed-squared scale because of the effects of air resistance.

energy required by exercise. (See chapter 1.) During anaerobic
metabolism, cells get their energy from glycogen (the stored
form of carbohydrate) rather than from blood glucose. As
glycogen goes through the process of forming ATP (the imme-

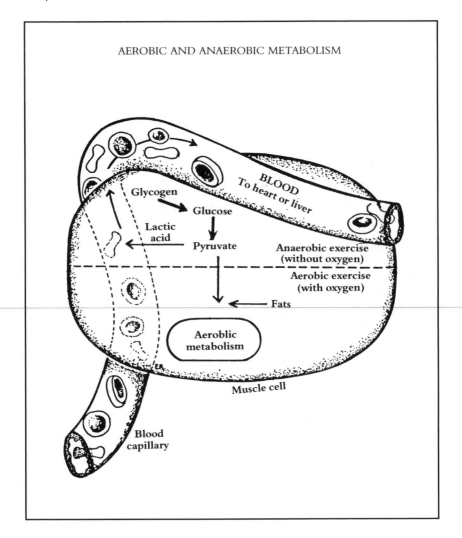

AEROBIC AND ANAEROBIC METABOLISM

During the metabolic process that creates energy for the muscle cell, glucose is converted to pyruvate. Oxygen is needed for the most effective continued metabolism and if not enough is present, lactic acid accumulates and can cause muscle pain.

diate energy source for cells), it breaks down into glucose, then pyruvate, and finally to lactic acid. When that's as far as the process can go because of lack of oxygen, the result is muscular pain. On the other hand, a sufficient supply of oxygen will allow some lactic acid to be burned and some to be converted back to glycogen. This is the relatively pain-free process of aerobic metabolism. (See illustration.)

A major factor in lactic acid build-up is exercise intensity. At about 60-70% of a rider's aerobic capacity, lactic acid production begins increasing. When a very high level of work or exercise is reached, lactic acid production becomes continuous.

At high lactic acid levels, muscular contraction is inhibited. This happens because proteins in muscle cells can function only within a certain range of acidity. Excess lactic acid simply shuts down cellular functions. The result is acute muscle fatigue. At this point you must stop exercising, or slow down. (Reminder: Always keep pedaling after a hard effort. Lactic acid is removed from the muscles and resynthesized more rapidly by light exercise than by rest.)

During exercise and for a time afterward, lactic acid escapes from the muscles into the blood. Blood levels of as high as 20 times the resting amount have been found after extreme anaerobic work. The exact fate of this excess lactic acid is not entirely understood. We do know that the liver removes some of it it from the blood. The liver also transforms lactic acid into glucose, which is either stored as glycogen or used as blood sugar. Through a complicated process, lactic acid is also used for fuel by the heart and muscle cells.

A study I performed with track cyclists yielded some clues as to how blood lactic acid build-up affects performance. The study involved 19 male riders, 13 of whom were current or past members of Olympic, Pan American, world championship, or national championship teams.

A blood sample was taken from each cyclist's arm five minutes after he completed his event. The five-minute wait allowed lactic acid to diffuse from the muscles to the blood and reach maximum levels. For comparison, samples were also obtained from four cyclists at rest.

Six samples were drawn after the 1,000-meter individual time trial, and 7 were taken after the match sprints. One cyclist was tested twice in the match sprints. After the team pursuit, 5 samples were drawn. Twelve samples were drawn during various rounds of the 4,000-meter individual pursuit: 2 individual pursuiters had 3 samples drawn, 1 gave 2 samples, and 4 gave 1 sample each.

The blood lactic acid values were recorded in millimoles per liter of blood (mM/l). (A mole is a given amount of chemical compound by weight. The weight depends upon the number and kind of atoms making up the compound.) A normal resting value for blood lactic acid is 1-2 mM/l, while values as high as 25-30 mM/l have been recorded after exhaustive exercise.

The results for the various events are shown in the table. The highest mean value for lactic acid, 16.94 mM/l, occurred

LACTIC ACID CONCENTRATIONS AFTER TRACK EVENTS

	Rest	Team pursuit	Match sprints	Individual pursuit	Kilometer
Number of samples	4	5	7	12	6
Mean lactate concentration (in mM/l)	1.95	12.08	13.65	15.18	16.94
Range of value	1.80-2.23	9.79-15.25	11.40-15.11	13.55-17.31	15.69-18.32
Mean time (seconds)		288	11	301.1	70.9

Tests on national caliber track cyclists show high levels of blood lactate five minutes after competition and indicate the differing anaerobic demands of the various events.

in the 1,000-meter time trial, an event which requires about 70 seconds of all-out riding. Small differences were found among the events. Team pursuiters had lower lactic acid concentrations, while values were higher in the match sprints (the shortest event) and in the individual pursuit (the longest).

You may be wondering why there is a relatively large amount of lactic acid in the blood after a match sprint, a race that requires only about 11 seconds of intense riding. Usually in events of 10 seconds, an athlete will use energy stored in the muscle and produce little lactic acid. After 10 seconds, glucose or glycogen must be broken down to produce ATP.

During the match sprint, the demand for ATP is so tremendous that not enough oxygen is available to produce it aerobically. Lactic acid results from anaerobic production and then is diffused into the blood. Previous research with athletes has shown that if the work intensity is sufficiently high, lactic acid can be produced within 10 seconds.

There is also some indication that the psychological stress involved in high-intensity exercise may increase lactic acid levels. This is attributed to the elevated activity of the nervous system and the increased secretion of adrenalin, which promotes the breakdown of glycogen and glucose.

Though we tend to think of match sprints as very short, high-intensity events, remember that the cyclist is on the track for several minutes under tremendous stress. The high adrenalin output probably causes the high lactic acid levels.

Research by Soviet scientists has shown improved performances by cyclists who face competitive situations many times during the season, which suggests that a rider can get used to the stress of competition.

The low lactic acid values in the team pursuit compared to the other events could be attributed to the short time each rider spends breaking the wind at the front of the line. By sharing the effort of overcoming wind resistance while traveling at

48 kph, the cyclist's required output was reduced 29-33%. By taking turns at the front, each rider uses less energy and can complete more of the work aerobically.

The next table shows values for subjects who had multiple samples drawn after individual pursuits. A low correlation was found between riding time and lactic acid concentration.

The low correlation between individual pursuit times and lactic acid concentration indicates that other variables may be important in predicting performance. The last-lap effort, wind direction, and state of aerobic conditioning may all play a part in the amount of lactic acid produced.

COMPARISON OF BLOOD LACTATE CONCENTRATIONS
AND PERFORMANCE TIMES

Cyclist	4,000-meter pursuit round	Blood actate (mM/l)	Time (sec.)
J.B.	Qualifying	13.73	298.8
	Quarter-finals	13.55	298.8
	Final	15.66	298.0
K.L.	Qualifying	14.25	301.3
	Quarter-finals	14.07	301.3
	Semi-finals	15.99	303.3
D.G.	Qualifying	16.09	301.2
	Quarter-finals	16.13	301.2
P.D.	Qualifying	17.13	314.2
E.H.	Qualifying	14.88	314.0
B.D.	Qualifying	15.93	308.4
G.P.	Qualifying	14.56	308.2

Is lactic acid build-up directly related to variations in performance time? Apparently not, according to these tests on individual pursuiters. Other factors such as wind direction and training level are probably also involved.

Can training make your muscles produce less lactic acid and tolerate it better? It appears so. When your aerobic capacity is increased with training you produce less lactic acid than you do when untrained. You are also better able to burn fat for fuel, a process that does not directly produce lactic acid. Also, during maximum efforts, you should be able to withstand higher lactic acid levels.

It takes time to repay oxygen debt

You've probably noticed that after you finish a long, hard jump, your demand for energy falls off but you continue to breathe rapidly. This is necessary to repay what is known as the oxygen debt.

The concept of oxygen debt is often misunderstood. The term is sometimes thought to mean that oxygen is borrowed from somewhere within the body. Actually, during maximum work the depletion of oxygen stored in muscle and blood amounts to only .06 liters. Oxygen debts as high as 30 times this amount have been found.

There are two components to oxygen debt — the alactacid oxygen debt, and the lactacid oxygen debt.

The alactacid oxygen debt refers to the large amount of oxygen that needs to be consumed during the first two or three minutes after hard exercise. This initial large quantity of oxygen is used to replenish the muscles' ATP-PC energy stores.

The lactacid oxygen debt refers to the oxygen needed to help transport lactic acid out of the muscles and convert it to blood glucose or stored glycogen. The lactacid oxygen debt can vary in size, ranging up to about eight liters. Researchers have found that following exhaustive exercise about 50% of the lactacid oxygen debt will be repaid in 15 minutes, 75% in 30 minutes, and about 95% in one hour.

So while the rapid breathing needed to repay the alactacid oxygen debt usually subsides after a few minutes, it can take much longer to fully recover from the lactacid oxygen debt. For example, after a hard effort, you should expect 2-3 minutes of rapid breathing to repay the alactacid oxygen debt, and between 30-60 minutes for full repayment of the lactacid oxygen debt.

3 / *Physiology and the female cyclist*

Historically, women cyclists have been slower overall than their male counterparts, as seen in the current U.S. men's and women's 40-km time trial records of 47:35:37 and 51:36:24, respectively. Does this discrepancy represent biological differences between the sexes, or does it reflect the social and cultural restrictions that women have grown up with? Just how do women cyclists compare to their male counterparts? Data on women cyclists is very limited, but general comparisons between male and female athletes can be made.

Does body fat help or hurt?

The female athlete's body composition varies considerably with every sport, but a woman typically has more body fat than a man. Most 18- to 22-year-old females average between 22% and 26% body fat, while males of the same age average 12-16%. My associates and I have found that top female cyclists have about 15% body fat, while males are in the 8-9% range. Compared to females in other sports, women cyclists have lower body fat than basketball players (20.8%), gymnasts (15.5%), and other varsity sports (20.6%).

Higher levels of androgen hormone (testosterone) in the male are undoubtedly responsible for his lower fat percentage. Similarly, higher levels of estrogen in the female are at least partially responsible for her greater fat weight. Women tend to have more fat in breasts, thighs, and hips, and a natural tendency to become fatter than men.

One popular theory hypothesizes that since women have a higher percentage of body fat and fat is an excellent source of fuel in endurance exercise, females should be able to metabolize it more efficiently and perform better in long-distance events. However, studies by exercise physiologist David Costill found that male and female runners with the same training mileage and the same max VO_2 had the same ability to burn fat. This means that when males and females work at the same relative percentage of maximum capacity, they will burn the same amounts of fats and carbohydrates.

Are women at a disadvantage when it comes to cooling systems, such as perspiration ability? When males and females with equal training backgrounds were compared it was found that both groups had the same sweating response. Actually, women have more sweat glands than men, which can be made even more efficient through training.

In terms of actual physical strength, women are not as strong as men, though this difference varies according to the area of the body. A woman's upper-body strength is 43-63% less than a man's, and lower-body strength is around 27% less. Strength is extremely important in events requiring rapid acceleration and speed. So women are at a relative disadvantage in road sprinting and track competition.

Both men and women can increase their strength, but men can achieve greater strength gains and muscle hypertrophy (excessive growth in size). Women can increase their strength up to 30% but with little or no sign of muscular hypertrophy because of the lower levels of testosterone in their systems.

In most sports, there is a considerable difference in max VO$_2$ between male and female athletes. Females usually have 15-30% less aerobic power than males. Studies with cyclists, however, indicate that in cycling the differences between the sexes are much smaller.

To a large degree, the difference in aerobic capacity between males and females is attributed to differences in hemoglobin concentration. (Hemoglobin is the oxygen-carrying component of the blood.) When hemoglobin concentration is the same, women appear equal to men.

Menstruation and training

One of the great debates about female performance in athletics concerns menstruation. Should women avoid exercise and competition during various phases of the menstrual cycle?

Women appear to differ greatly with regard to exercise and competition during menstruation. Many have few or no menstrual difficulties or irregularities under any conditions, whether they are active or sedentary. On the other hand, a significant number of women have difficulties that are neither helped nor aggravated by vigorous activity.

Several recent medical surveys have revealed that female athletes have a higher degree of menstrual irregularites and cessation of menstruation (amenorrhea) than the general population of women. Many people think exercise is the cause of this, but this is not necessarily the case.

As any athlete knows, when you begin training seriously, you may experience a change in diet and sleeping patterns, a decrease in body fat, and possible physical and emotional stress. When you try to coordinate social and professional responsibilities with cycling you may find that the level of stress increases still further. Exercise and emotional stress produce both immediate and long-term changes in the body's hormone concentrations. Some hormones are produced in response to stress, and they may in turn trigger the release of additional hormones. It can be extremely difficult to isolate any one of these variables to determine its effect on menstrual irregularities.

Every month hormones from the pituitary gland in the brain initiate the menstrual cycle. Two of these hormones, luteinizing hormone and follicle-stimulating hormone, combine to mature an ovarian follicle, the casing that houses the egg in the ovary. Estrogen levels in the blood also increase at this time.

This huge estrogen rise triggers an increase in luteinizing secretion, which in turn triggers ovulation. During ovulation (around the 14th day of the cycle), the mature egg ruptures the ovarian follicle, from which it then emerges, and migrates through the fallopian tubes into the uterus. The remnant of the ovarian follicle begins to secrete estrogen and progesterone, which together prepare the lining of the uterus for implantation of a fertilized egg. If fertilization does not take place by the 22nd or 23rd day of the cycle, the uterine lining begins to atrophy. The estrogen and progesterone levels markedly decrease, the uterine lining sloughs off, and vaginal bleeding follows, normally lasting from three to seven days.

It is well known that amenorrhea can occur in extremely thin women or women who lose large amounts of body fat. It has also been shown that estrogen is metabolized differently in these women. Some of the differences in metabolism may produce alterations in the way various glands function, particularly the pituitary gland and the ovaries, and these changes may result in menstrual disturbances.

Exercise, too, may have an effect on menstrual function. Hormones released by the brain (endorphins) may decrease the levels of hormones needed for normal menstrual function. Endorphins are released during exercise and this may be a possible link between these hormones and amenorrhea.

With no concrete evidence that exercise is the main cause of amenorrhea, a cyclist with menstrual problems should continue training but seek medical advice from a gynecologist who knows the importance of exercise. It should never be assumed that only training is causing the problem.

Causes of menstrual cramps

Menstrual cramps are caused by the muscles of the uterus contracting in response to a substance called prostaglandin. A few days preceding menstruation, when progesterone levels suddenly drop off, the prostaglandin level rises, triggering uterine contractions. The prostaglandins also affect other smooth muscles in the pelvic cavity and are thought to cause contractions of the intestine, stomach, and certain blood vessels. This is a normal process, but unfortunately some women produce too much prostaglandin.

Many women with painful menstruation (dysmenorrhea) can be helped with new anti-inflammatory medications that inhibit the production of cramp-producing prostaglandins, such as ibuprofen (brand name Motrin, Advil), naproxen (naprosyn), naproxen sodium (Anaprox) and mefenamic acid (Ponstel). Along with the decreased prostaglandins in the pelvic cavity, there is less uterine contraction, and the side effects of nausea, vomiting, and headaches are dramatically reduced.

Many athletes have reported a reduction in menstrual cramps after becoming active in their sport. Research has not led to any firm conclusions as to why this happens. One possibility may be the release of endorphins, which act as natural pain killers and relieve the pain of cramping. Also, because of the nature of their efforts, athletes may simply be able to tolerate more pain.

But don't expect a vigorous cycling program to provide total relief from menstrual cramps. And remember, just because your pain is reduced while exercising doesn't mean that doubling the exercise will double the relief.

Exercise and delayed puberty

Many people believe that athletes enter puberty at a later age than their sedentary counterparts. They hypothesize that arduous training prior to the onset of menstruation (menarche) does not allow the endocrine (hormone) system to develop normally.

The fact that some females who were very active as children also had delayed menarche does not establish cause and effect. It is conceivable, however, that delayed menarche will lead to greater athletic success. It has been shown that girls with early onset of puberty are usually shorter and fatter. Delayed menarche may produce a taller and leaner woman with a better chance of success in sport. This is only an hypothesis; the whole issue deserves further research.

Training during pregnancy

To my knowledge, no studies on humans have shown any harmful effects of training during pregnancy. And physically fit women may withstand the rigors of labor better than sedentary ones.

With some modifications in their program, such as a slower pace because of the added workload, pregnant cyclists can continue to train. Discuss your training and exercise program with your obstetrician for adaptation to your particular pregnancy. If any problems arise (pain, bleeding, etc.) see your doctor immediately for advice on what can be done safely.

If you're pregnant, you should exercise in the coolest part of the day. Don't let your body temperature exceed 101 degrees, since heat has been implicated in certain birth defects. Prolonged heat exposure can also lead to premature labor. Take your temperature after exercise and, if necessary, wear lighter clothing or ride shorter distances.

In my opinion, racing should be avoided because of the possibility of an accident and the increased metabolic effort and consequently increased body temperature associated with competition.

Endurance training, debunking the myths

Should women train differently than men? Though it is generally true that women have less blood, a smaller heart in relation to body mass, lower hemoglobin levels, and a smaller heart stroke volume than men, both sexes can significantly improve oxygen transport through training, thereby increasing their ability to exercise for extended periods. Research indicates that females respond to endurance training in the same way as males.

Women usually do race shorter distances than men for reasons based on politics and superstition, not physiology. In international cycling government, conservatism and lack of understanding have limited the distance of the women's world championship road race to 110 km (66 miles) and stage races to 12 days. However, based on research and available evidence, there appears to be no scientific support for different treatment of men and women.

For many years women were kept from endurance events on the grounds that they could not tolerate heat stress over extended periods. Many of these misconceptions were fostered by poorly designed studies in which researchers used trained men and sedentary women performing tasks that might be moderate for males but significantly harder for females.

A woman's fitness level will dictate how well she will adapt and respond to heat stress. A trained female cyclist will be able to increase her heart rate enough to prevent a drop in blood pressure when blood is redistributed to the skin for heat dispersion. Remember that for women, as well as for men, acclimatization also increases heat tolerance.

TRAINING

4 / Determining your training needs

You're out with your local bike club on a group training ride. For most of the 40 miles you have no trouble maintaining the steady, 20 mph pace. But suddenly one of the lead riders accelerates and you drop off the back of the pack. You're left to limp back to the starting point on your own.

What happened? Clearly you had the endurance to keep up with the pack. What you lacked was the anaerobic capacity to cover the frequent shifts in tempo that are part of every group training ride or race.

Energy needs depend on event

Your training should include aerobic and anaerobic work because bicycle racing requires both. One key to developing an effective training plan is to understand how aerobic and anaerobic ability relate to a given event. Once you know, you can design your workouts to bring about optimum conditioning.

The first table shows various cycling events and the primary energy sources used in them. For example, match sprinters' most important source is the ATP-PC system, which provides high energy for a very short time. Pursuiters, on the other hand, depend on the anaerobic (lactic acid) system, while road

ENERGY USED IN CYCLING EVENTS

		Percentage of time spent		
	Performance time	Speed (ATP-PC strength)	Anaerobic capacity (speed and lactic acid system)	Aerobic capacity (oxygen system)
	Hours : minutes			
100-mile road race	3:55 - 4:10	—	5	95
100-kilometer criterium	2:05 - 2:15	5	10	85
100-kilometer team time trial	2:10 - 2:20	—	15	85
25-mile time trial	0:52 - 0:60	—	10	90
25-mile criterium	0:50 - 0:60	5	15	80
	Minutes : seconds			
10-mile track	20:00 - 25:00	10	20	70
4,000-meter individual pursuit	4:45 - 5:05	20	55	25
Kilometer	1:07 - 1:13	80	15	5
Match sprints	0:11 - 0:13	98	2	—

You can design a training program using this guide to the energy systems used in your event. Road races, for example, make greater demands on the aerobic system than track events.

racers rely primarily on the aerobic system. (For more on these energy systems see chapter 2.)

You can develop these three energy sources by manipulating the intensity and duration of your training. The principle of specificity applies — you become good at doing what you train to do.

Be aware that some of the percentages indicated on the chart may be deceptive, especially for the long road events. For example, you may be tempted to dismiss the 5% anaerobic requirement in the 100-mile road race as something not worth training for. But think about it for a moment. If that road race lasts 250 minutes (4 hours and 10 minutes), 5% is 12.5 minutes. That's a long time to be using anaerobic energy sources. It can't be done without appropriate training.

For hard efforts lasting up to two minutes, anaerobic power is most important. At about two minutes, there is a 50:50 ratio of anaerobic to aerobic. As the duration of the work increases, aerobic power takes on greater importance. To illustrate this, the graph shows the energy yield from aerobic and anaerobic processes during a 60-minute maximal effort.

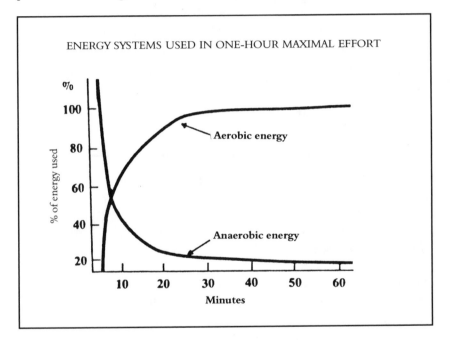

ENERGY SYSTEMS USED IN ONE-HOUR MAXIMAL EFFORT

The energy yield from anaerobic metabolism is greatest in the first few minutes of an all-out effort. After about 20 minutes more than 80% of energy used comes from aerobic processes.

Even for events where the percentage of anaerobic work is low, your training should include some anaerobic work (unless you're able to race more than once a week, which will serve as a substitute). Such training will help you develop the ability to chase back to the pack after a tire puncture, bridge from group to group, attack to break away, climb strongly, or sprint for the finish line.

The second table shows the effect of various types of training on aerobic and anaerobic capacity. Refer to the first table for the requirements of your event and then to the second one for the training method to use.

How should you train if you compete in several different kinds of events? Use a combination of training methods until you're ready to peak for a specific road race, criterium, time trial, or track event. Then, with three or four weeks to go, concentrate on the one or two types of training that are ideal for the event.

Here's a description of each of the workouts listed in the table.

ENERGY SYSTEMS DEVELOPED BY TRAINING METHODS

Types of training	% Anaerobic capacity	% Aerobic capacity
Sprint training	95	5
Acceleration sprints	90	10
Set sprints	80	20
Intervals	50	50
Speed play (Fartlek)	50	50
Repetition riding	60	40
Continuous fast riding	15	85
Continuous slow riding	5	95

Once you know the energy systems used in the various segments of your event, you can use this table as a guide to the types of training that will help develop them.

Sprint training: A series of short sprints (50-75 meters) ridden at maximum speed. This develops the ATP-PC energy systems.

Acceleration sprints: A gradual increase from a slow speed to an all-out effort, covering about 150 meters. This will improve both speed and endurance. (It is the safest speed training in cold weather because you reach your maximum effort gradually, lessening the risk of muscle injury.)

Set sprints: A progressive series of sprints alternated with short periods of recovery. For example, sprint 50 meters, ride medium pace for 50 meters; sprint 50 meters, ride slow for 50 meters; sprint 75, ride medium for 75; sprint 75, ride slow 75; sprint 100, ride medium 100; sprint 100, ride slow 100. This training develops speed and endurance.

Intervals: A series of short efforts of equal length, alternated with periods of easier riding that allow a certain degree of recovery. There are two types of intervals, slow and fast.

Slow intervals are ridden slower than race pace, with short recovery periods. For example, 20 500-meter efforts with 30 seconds of easy pedaling between each one. This workout will improve endurance fitness but won't do much for speed.

Fast intervals are ridden as fast or faster than your average race speed, producing a heart rate around 185. Recovery periods are long enough to let your pulse drop almost to normal. For example, 20 500-meter efforts with 2-minute rest intervals. This training helps you withstand fatigue in the absence of oxygen. In other words, it develops your anaerobic systems.

Speed play: A concept popular in running, where it's known by the Swedish term *fartlek*, speed play is unstructured training that incorporates all the training methods described above. It requires riding fairly long distances at various paces, so it's most appropriate for road races. The absence of rigid structure is psychologically stimulating — the rider has the freedom to decide when and how he will make the hard efforts. A *fartlek* workout can also be planned in advance. For example, 5-mile warm-up; 5 50-meter hard efforts with 60-second rest intervals; 5 miles at 75% effort; 4 acceleration sprints of 75 meters; 4 1,000-meter efforts faster than race pace with an easy 1,000 meters after each; 5 miles at medium pace; 8 50-meter efforts at almost full effort with an easy 150 meters between each; 10 miles at 50-75% effort; 4 times hard up a short hill with easy riding back down; 5 easy miles for cooling down.

Repetition riding: Covering distances of 1,000-2,000 meters at a speed close to race pace with rest periods long enough to allow almost complete recovery. Of course, the longer the distance, the slower the speed. A 4,000-meter pursuiter may ride at or near maximum pace for 2,000 meters, with complete recovery between efforts. This type of training works on the anaerobic systems.

Continuous fast riding: Training distance is slightly greater than race distance, while speed is the same or only slightly slower than race pace. For example, a 3,000-meter pursuiter may ride 3,500-4,000 meters several times, with rest periods of 5-10 minutes. This training builds endurance and will gradually condition the body to race pace.

Continuous slow riding: The speed is slower than race pace, and distance is proportional to the event. A sprinter may ride 25 miles, while a road racer may cover 100-125 miles. This type of training is widely known as long, steady distance (LSD). The greatest benefit of LSD is aerobic endurance.

Specific training: Divide and conquer

How do you tailor workouts to your particular event? Start by dividing the event into segments and then train to develop the energy source needed for each segment. For example, the 1,000-meter time trial can be divided into three segments. Explosive power is necessary to get the pedals turning quickly in the first few meters. Acceleration takes the rider to maximum speed. Aerobic capacity dictates how long he can hold that maximum speed and avoid slowing down at the end of the event.

In terms of energy sources needed, the ATP-PC system is used during the explosive power and acceleration parts of the event. Then it's up to the lactic acid system to get the rider to the finish.

Train for each segment independently of the others. This means practicing each part of the ride several times. Some kilometer time trial riders make the mistake of always training at the full distance. As a result, after several rides they have little energy left for a rewarding workout. They would be better off repeating certain parts of the total race.

As the competitive season nears, begin putting two or more segments of the event together. Continue adding segments until you are doing the entire event.

How much does that layoff cost you?

As riders begin preseason training, their fundamental questions are: "How much physical fitness have I lost during the winter?" and, "Which body systems have deteriorated most?" It would be great to have the answers at the very start of training. Then you could devise a specific workout program to make up for the losses, and so save both time and needless effort.

Unfortunately, the answers are hard to come by. Many riders fall into the trap of thinking, "If some training is good, more must be better." Even some skilled coaches, who know how to train specific abilities in athletes, have a hard time knowing where immediate attention is needed.

Compounding the problem is the fact that no two cyclists are the same. Racers differ in mind and body build, and no one gains or loses athletic efficiency according to a specific time-table. As three-time Tour de France winner Greg LeMond says, athletes are not programmable.

How fast do physical systems decline? It's difficult to say. In general, it appears that individuals who stay fairly active during the off-season see a gradual decline. Complete inactivity usually results in rapid loss.

A study I participated in provided some further insights. We studied 16 competitive cyclists at Florida State University to determine how they had been affected by the winter layoff. In general, we found that the layoff had not greatly harmed the response of the cyclists' cardiovascular systems to high levels of work. A mean max VO_2 value of 4.28 liters per minute during February indicated that the cyclists had not been inactive during the off-season months. Apparently, engaging in endurance activities such as hiking, mountain bike riding, bicycle touring, cross-country skiing, and ice skating provides enough cardiovascular stimulation to prevent a serious decline in oxygen uptake from the previous season's high.

This means that if a cyclist knows his max VO_2, and it's relatively good, he may not have to unduly restrict himself to a long, slow distance schedule early in the season. Instead he could begin training that would ordinarily come later in the season, such as climbing, speedwork, intervals, time trials, etc.

The test subjects exhibited a rather low value for anaerobic power. Because this was an early season assessment, we attributed the low value to two things: a lack of sufficient training stimulus such as intervals, and the general emphasis on endurance training early in the year.

We also took a look at another common effect of a winter layoff — weight gain. Our 16 cyclists had an average weight of 146 pounds (66.5 kg). Almost 17 pounds (8 kg) or 11.6% of this was fat weight. This is about 2% more fat weight than is normally seen in top competitive male cyclists.

Measurements of lung function told us a lot about the efficiency of the respiratory system. Our group recorded excellent values for all pulmonary tests, reaffirming findings that lungs don't lose their high functional capacity quickly. Therefore, it is probably not necessary for cyclists to do specific off-season exercises to maintain or improve the muscles associated with breathing. Previous training and competition will have provided the stimulation necessary to keep the respiratory system in good working order. This is not to imply, however, that the respiratory system will take care of itself over an extended layoff of more than three or four months.

Based on our findings, these are the factors you should consider during preseason training.

— Loss of fitness does take place during the winter layoff, but the loss can be minimized by any physical activities that challenge the body's organ systems.
— Every individual responds differently to training. Also, individuals differ in the degree of fitness they lose because of the winter layoff. So an assessment of your physiological functions is essential early in the season to pinpoint deficiencies. That way, you can make more profitable use of your training time and make a more rapid return to competitive fitness.

Lab tests pinpoint fitness frailties

Athletes and coaches in many sports are finding the results of lab tests helpful in developing training programs. For example, if a cyclist is found to have limited oxygen-transporting power, long-distance riding can be prescribed to build up the heart and lungs. Another rider, overweight at the beginning of the season can be correctly advised on how much fat to lose.

For years U.S. coaches and exercise physiologists used various tests to try to assess a rider's physical fitness and potential. The lack of standardization made it difficult to compare Americans with each other and with riders from other countries. In the last few years, however, the following tests have become standard procedure and will give you a good foundation from which to develop your training plan.

Where can you have such testing done? Many universities have exercise physiology labs and they need well-conditioned athletes for research. More and more riders are being tested at the Olympic Training Center during training camps in Colorado Springs, Colorado. YMCAs and private fitness centers are also good places. If you go to a private testing service, be prepared to pay $100-$300.

Body composition

Your lung capacity, body fat percentage, kilograms of fat, lean body mass, and total weight should all be recorded. Your body composition should be determined so you'll know if you need to lose weight after the winter layoff and how low you can safely go during the season. (For more information on body composition testing, see chapter 8.)

Lung volume

Lung measurements, done with a standard bell spirometer or computerized spirometer, should include the following: forced vital capacity (total volume of air that can be expelled following full inspiration), forced expiratory flow in one second, forced expiratory flow at 25% and 75% of expiration, and maximum voluntary ventilation. These measurements indicate total lung volume. By measuring air exchange during a single maximum breath, they assess the strength of the respiratory muscles.

Explosive leg power

Explosive leg power is associated with anaerobic energy production, a prime factor in cycling success. There are three tests that measure it.

— Magaria-Kalaman power test. This is an excellent indicator of explosive power. The cyclist stands six meters in front of a staircase then runs up the stairs as fast as possible, taking three steps at a time. Electronic mats or photoelectric cells are placed on the third and ninth steps and connected to a timer that measures to the hundredth of a second. The test is administered several times and the fastest performance is recorded. Results are reported in power measurements, similar to horsepower.

— Isokinetic test. A device known as the Cybex II evaluates strength, power, and endurance in the muscles of the knees and hips. Cybex II measures muscular output at preselected and controlled velocities, from isometric (0 degrees per second) to fast speeds (up to 300 degrees per second). Strength is determined by a single extension and flexion of the muscles at increasing speeds. Power and endurance are determined in a 45-second contraction test.

— Bicycle power (anaerobic) test. This measures power output on the bicycle ergometer. After a 3-minute warm-up at 90 rpm, the load is rapidly increased to 7 kilopounds, and the rider does everything possible to maintain pedal speed, including standing up. The test ends when cadence drops below 75 rpm. Total riding time is recorded and post-exercise blood lactic acid is analyzed. This test determines the ability to produce high power output for short periods of time, plus tolerance to lactic acid build-up in muscles.

Cardiorespiratory evaluation

Two tests help determine aerobic and anaerobic fitness. The first is done on a bicycle ergometer equipped with dropped handlebars, toe clips, and a racing saddle. The second requires a road bicycle on a motor-driven treadmill. Both tests assess how the circulatory and respiratory systems adapt to training and how they use energy stores during prolonged, high-intensity exercise.

The first test measures your maximal oxygen consumption (max VO_2). It consists of continuous pedaling on the ergometer at a steady cadence, usually around 90 rpm, while the resistance is progressively increased. The test ends when the rider is no longer able to maintain a cadence of 90.

The second test simulates actual riding conditions by using a treadmill set at 20 mph. The grade is increased 0.5% each minute from an initial setting of 2% or 3%. The following measurements are recorded each minute: oxygen consumption, pulmonary ventilation, respiratory quotient, ventilatory equivalent, heart rate, and oxygen pulse.

Overtraining: How to Spot and Avoid It

The main worry of any competitive cyclist is not injury but overtraining. They are not worried about pulled muscles, stress fractures or crashing but fatigue and exhaustion and that "out of gas feeling" in the closing home stretch of the race. Most experienced coaches and athletes know that you can lose races by training too much rather than too little. They also recognize the temptation to forego a program of building and pacing training, and instead go by the adage, "What doesn't destroy me, makes me stronger."

The phenomenon of overtraining, staleness, burnout or fatigue is very real. Considering the high demands placed on today's athletes in school, by family commitments and the length of the cycling season, it is not surprising that many cyclists need to keep an eye out for staleness and symptoms of overtraining (Appendix 1).

In *The Lore of Running*, Dr. Tim Noakes gives examples of several nationally ranked athletes with training induced over-training symptoms. One athlete exhibited the classic physical and psychological signs when he complained that he was lethargic, sleeping poorly, his morning pulse had increased by 10 beats and he had less enthusiasm for training and particularly competition. He expressed concern that his legs felt "sore" and "heavy" and that the feeling had lasted for several training sessions. Another distance runner reported that three weeks after a marathon he was still sleeping poorly, had a persistent sore throat, and felt like his energy level was constantly low. These two athletes were exhibiting the classic signs and symptoms of overtraining, and were in urgent need of complete rest from hard training.

You can see the symptoms of overtraining in an athlete who is eager to excel, and begins to train frequently and intensely. At first the athlete improves, but after a while training times become static and below their set goals. Eager to pass the dead point, the athlete begins to train even harder. Instead of improving, times become worse and a sense of inadequacy and frustration develops. Besides declines in performance, some changes in personality and behavior are detected. The athlete has developed a state of staleness, chronic fatigue or overtraining. (See Appendix 1 for more on symptoms of staleness.)

Physiological Indicators to Monitor

In the early 1980's, Dick Brown, who at the time was an administrator/physiologist of Athletics West (world class running club), conducted a project on athletes to try to identify potential indicators of overtraining. Of the several dozen indicators monitored, three were found to be of use to the athletes in their daily training and could be recorded in their training diaries without expensive laboratory monitoring equipment. These were: morning body weight, morning heart rate, and hours of sleep.

His research pointed out that if an athlete's morning heart rate was 10 percent or higher, if the athlete received 10 percent less sleep, or if the athlete's weight was down 3 percent or more, the athlete's body was sending a signal: either it had not recovered from the previous hard workout, or some form of illness was plaguing the athlete. Brown's research points out that an athlete should cut back on his day's workout if they are abnormal in two indicators and it may be best to take the day off if they register in the red in all three indicators. This is the time to use an hour of that training time for a nap.

Hans Selye, a researcher, stated in his classic text, *The Stress of Life*, that every person has only so much adaptive energy to use against stress. If an athlete uses much of their physical and mental energy for other matters in their daily lives, they will have less energy for training and competition. Consequently, they will not be able to adapt to the stress of the sport. The only way out is to ensure adequate rest and sleep, remove or decrease the other stress factors, or decrease training.

Discussions of stress (overtraining) usually end with the same statement: too little stress, physical or psychological, does not bring about desired changes; too much stress is harmful. But by knowing your body's warning signals and the stages of adaptation, you can train smart and steadily improve your fitness.

Numbers tell the story on overtraining

One way to tell if you're overtraining is through blood testing. Done frequently, such tests can spot infection and symptoms of fatigue before they hurt your performance.

Blood tests can be peformed on the referral of a physician at any hospital or clinic. To get the most accurate results, rest at least one day after a hard training session or race, and drink enough liquids to be at normal body weight. Though blood tests are somewhat expensive, they are a worthwhile part of your preseason physical, and anytime you go through an extended bad period during the season, a test can help determine the cause.

The blood constituents used in the identification of over-training are:

— Red blood cells. These supply oxygen to working cells and remove waste products. The normal value for males is 4-6 million per cubic millimeter of blood; females have slightly lower counts. Low values are seen when there is anemia, severe infection, or loss of blood. High values indicate dehydration or certain kidney diseases.

— Hemoglobin. This is the iron protein substance located within red blood cells. Its primary function is to transport oxygen from the lungs to body tissues. Serum hemoglobin increases when red blood cells are destroyed, and a high count indicates certain blood ailments, such as sickle cell anemia. Low levels occur after a large blood loss and sometimes as a result of intensive training. Normal hemoglobin levels are 14-18 grams per 100 milliliters of blood in men and 12-15 grams in women.

— Hematocrit. This is the percentage of red blood cells in the total blood volume. A blood sample is centrifuged to force solid matter to the bottom of a specially marked tube, leaving clear plasma in the upper section. The test measures the thickness of the blood as well as the amount of fluid in the blood. Low values are seen in cases of excessive fluid intake, severe bleeding, and red-blood-cell anemia. High concentrations of red cells can occur after exercise in hot weather because sweating causes loss of fluid from the plasma. Normal values are 45-55% in men and slightly lower in women.

— White blood cells. These increase in number when the body is fighting infections or inflammations. The cells help destroy the agents causing the infection. A count includes five types of white blood cells, which are formed and stored in the bone marrow, lymph glands, and spleen. The normal range is 5,000-10,000 per cubic millimeter of blood. Emotional stress can raise the white cell count, so you should be as relaxed as possible before the blood drawing.

The constituents of blood are critical to cycling performance. Since hemoglobin carries oxygen, it is obvious that the number of red blood cells and the amount of hemoglobin in those cells help determine how much oxygen can be supplied to working muscles. Blood also carries away lactic acid, carbon dioxide, and other by-products of metabolism.

It's not easy to predict how blood will change after a single ride or a period of training. Normal at-rest values for most blood constituents range widely. The ranges increase with exercise because of variations in training programs. Also, different methods of blood analysis produce slightly different results, and all athletes do not respond to exercise in the same manner. Each rider's test results should be compared only to his own normal values.

A study of elite male swimmers provides some clues as to how blood tests help monitor the effectiveness of training. Nine swimmers were tested during a period of hard training, tapering, and rest. The researchers looked for changes in hematocrit and hemoglobin.

During the hard training period there were 11 workouts each week. Each day's distance totaled 11,000-13,000 meters. Blood was drawn twice a week and, after analysis, the following observations were made:

— Heavy training had a detrimental effect on both hemoglobin and hematocrit values. During the period of hard work, hemoglobin values were below those recorded for males in general.
— All swimmers had a recovery in hemoglobin during the taper phase of their training.
— Of seven swimmers who were measured after competition (following the taper), six recorded higher values of hemoglobin and hematocrit than while in the taper.

The correlation between hemoglobin and hematocrit was moderate to low, so it was concluded that hematocrit was not a sensitive index of response to training. Researchers also determined that blood test results should be judged on an individual basis, since the swimmers exhibited a wide range of values.

This study shows that hemoglobin decreases during hard training, so hemoglobin recovery is a good index of an athlete's recovery. (Because of such fluctuations, an athlete's hemoglobin count may be misleading if it is compared with that of the average male population.)

Overtraining is a real phenomenon in cyclists and other endurance athletes. Measurements of various blood chemistries and counts can be useful in determining the onset of overtraining and recovery from it.

Training diary reveals weaknesses

Another way to monitor overtraining is to keep an accurate account of your exercise program. A training diary can provide a wealth of information and can reveal how your training program is either succeeding or failing.

Record everything that is pertinent to your riding performance — the more detailed the better. You can use one of the training diaries published specifically for this purpose or you can devise one of your own. Here are some things you might want to keep track of:

— Body weight. Record after a trip to the bathroom in the morning.
— Pulse. Count for 15 seconds in bed right after waking up. Count again after being up and around for a couple of minutes. Then find the difference between the two readings. Record all three numbers.
— Training. Write down the distance and elapsed time of the ride, the time you started, weather conditions and temperature, gears used, how you felt physically, and your degree of enthusiasm.
— Mechanical notes. If you do some bike maintenance or make an equipment change, put it down so you'll remember it. The same goes for alterations in riding position. It will help you pinpoint the cause of subsequent problems. A sore knee, for example, might not show up for days or even weeks after you moved the saddle or changed your cleats. Without a reminder

you might assume the cause is something that happened on the last ride.

— Diet. Be concerned mainly with diet trends or changes from the norm — things like missed meals or a poor variety of foods — which can be responsible for a decreased energy level.

— Stress. Problems with the job, school, or family can physically drain you. So can loss of sleep for any reason. Note any stress factors that might be hurting your performance on the bike.

The numbers provided by the morning checks — weight and pulse — are valuable in two ways. First they provide a day-to-day monitoring of your body and will tip you off to overtraining. For example, when the in-bed pulse or the pulse difference is suddenly 8 or 10 beats above your norm, it's a sign you haven't recovered from previous efforts. Adjust your training accordingly: either take the day off or train lightly. Also, if your weight drops several pounds in a day or two, you're becoming dehydrated and this will cause fatigue. Drink more before, during, and after rides.

The morning numbers are also valuable in the long haul, by giving you an objective indicator of when you're reaching peak fitness. By matching your subjective feelings of fitness and your on-bike performance with your morning readings, you can determine the numbers that pinpoint when you're really going well. Then it's a matter of training in a way that will keep those readings constant.

One thing about pulse readings — don't think twice about how yours compares with anyone else's. Every individual's is different. What matters is how yours behaves.

If the signs of overtraining are present, you may have to spend days or even weeks getting back to the level of fitness you just passed. So the best treatment is prevention.

Overtraining can be prevented

Here are some guidelines to help you avoid overtraining:

— Before progressing to hard training, do 8-10 weeks of endurance work to build a good aerobic base.
— Sleep at least eight hours each night.
— Eat a diet that supplies all the basic nutrients.
— If possible, take a 15-30 minute nap before afternoon workouts.
— Individualize speed workouts — the proper pace is what your own body can handle.
— Immediately before any major competition, especially stage races, reduce your training load for several days to increase physical and mental reserves for the big effort.

5 / Fine tuning

You've reached a plateau in your riding. Endurance is no problem — you feel like you can go all day — but you don't seem to be getting any faster. You add more miles to your weekly schedule, but your cycling computer still won't average more than 22 mph.

Interval training boosts speed

How do you go about increasing overall speed? The answer is interval training.

The term "interval training" is often abused and misused. Many cyclists mistakenly think it means any fast riding that is interspersed with slow riding. This is actually much closer to the definition of *fartlek* training, which is based on random efforts of various lengths and intensities. (See chapter 4.)

Interval training, on the other hand, is tightly structured. It has a preplanned number of efforts as well as a set duration for each one and for each rest period that follows. This makes it possible to change the stress of the workout by precise degrees.

Because it includes rest periods, interval training allows hard work with less painful accumulation of lactic acid than would normally occur with continuous high-intensity training. Without rest periods, the muscle fatigue caused by lactic acid quickly puts a stop to exercise. Because it spares you from such fatigue, interval training allows greater intensity or duration of workouts.

Interval training also improves heart stroke volume. (See chart.) During the rest or relief intervals, more blood is returned to the heart than would be the case during continuous exercise (when blood is needed by the muscles). The greater the amount of blood filling the heart, the greater the ability to contract and the larger the stroke volume. Increased stroke volume improves the flow of oxygen to working muscles.

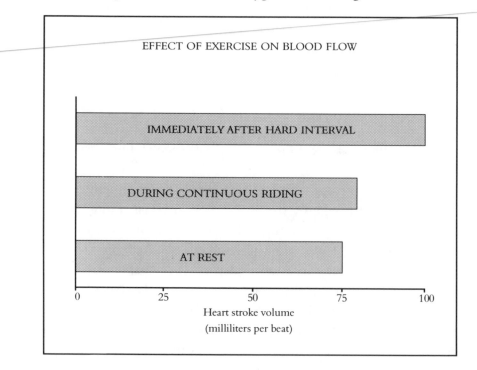

EFFECT OF EXERCISE ON BLOOD FLOW

IMMEDIATELY AFTER HARD INTERVAL

DURING CONTINUOUS RIDING

AT REST

0   25   50   75   100

Heart stroke volume
(milliliters per beat)

More intense than continuous riding, interval training increases heart stroke volume, which improves the flow of oxygen to the muscles.

During interval training the stroke volume reaches its max-imum level many times, thanks to all the rest periods.

There are several variables in interval training, any of which can be altered to adjust the stress of the workout, including:

— Work interval: the portion of the training when hard effort is made.
— Relief interval: (also called rest or recovery): the time spent between work intervals. It may consist of very easy pedaling, or moderate pedaling that requires some effort. The relief interval can be expressed as a ratio, such as 1:2. This means that the length of the rest is twice that of the work. When work intervals are long, the ratio is usually 1:1/2 or 1:1. It may be 1:2 for medium-length work intervals. During short, high-intensity intervals, a 1:3 ratio is frequently used.
— Set: a group of work and relief intervals. For example, five 200-meter sprints with predetermined pace and rest periods.
— Repetition: a single work interval. In the above set there are five repetitions.
— Training time: the period in which each repetition is to be completed. For example, 14 seconds for each 200-meter sprint.
— Training distance: the amount of ground covered during the work interval.

Here's how a coach would write down an interval workout for his riders: Set 1, 5×200 at 0:14 (0:45). In this formula, 5 is the number of repetitions, 200 is the training distance in meters, 0:14 is the training time in minutes and seconds, and 0:45 is the length of the relief intervals in minutes and seconds.

How much is enough

"How do I know whether my interval effort is too hard or not hard enough?" is a question riders frequently ask. There are two ways to determine proper intensity. One is by monitoring your heart rate, which is an excellent indicator. Use a wireless heart rate monitor such as a POLAR to accurately measure your heart rate during exercise. I suggest one that mounts on the bars but also can be worn on the wrist for cross-training purposes. In high-intensity training, a work interval should yield a heart rate of 170-180 beats per minute or slightly higher. As you become more fit, you will have to work harder to reach and maintain a high pulse.

The second tip-off to your effort level is the number of work intervals you can do in each training session. If you can't perform the full number of repetitions because of exhaustion, the effort was too hard. On the other hand, if it seems like you could easily do several more repetitions, the effort was not hard enough.

Pedal easily during the relief intervals. This promotes the return of blood from muscles to the heart while allowing the ATP-PC system to regenerate. When doing longer intervals to stress the aerobic system, there should be a moderate effort during the rest periods. When you wish to stress the lactic acid system, ride harder during recovery.

You can use your heart rate to judge when it's time to begin the next repetition or set. In general, once your pulse falls to 130-140 beats per minute, you're ready to begin the next work interval. Let it drop to 120 beats per minute between the end of one set and the beginning of the next. (This method works well if you have a cycling computer that has a heart rate function.)

Interval training shouldn't be done more than twice a week by mature cyclists or once a week by beginners. Why the caution, since there seem to be so many advantages? Interval training is hard work that increases the possibility of injury. Too many intervals increase the risk of strained muscles and joints. Also, the constant repetition of short distances invites mental staleness.

Finally, although interval training is essential for some purposes, it does not provide total conditioning or the necessary skills for long criteriums and road races. Long-distance training and rides at close to race pace are needed to fully develop your muscular and cardiovascular capacity.

Bicycle road racing is a fast, continuous activity that intermittently requires periods of great effort. Interval training can help you meet this tough double challenge.

Getting faster takes practice

While many riders may have the endurance to ride any major event, some lack the speed it takes when the final sprint comes. I think we Americans put too much distance in our training, at the expense of speed and technique.

The reason has to do with fear of or a reluctance to deal with speed. For most cyclists, it's a lot simpler to increase total mileage than to work out a balance between speed, technique, and distance training.

But if you want to become faster, you must practice cycling faster. If two riders have comparable natural speed, the one who practices sprinting will win. Even simple speedwork and sprinting will help, but in-depth results come only from training that concentrates on speed. (Remember that no high-intensity training should be done without a firm base of conditioning miles. This is especially critical for young riders.)

What's the difference between speedwork and intervals? In speedwork, you keep the distances short to maintain speed.

With intervals, the distances may be longer, but the intensity or speed is not as great.

Here's an example of an excellent speed workout that covers a total of 40 miles, including 6 to 8 of progressively shorter work periods. All the work periods are performed at maximum speed. Rest periods consist of riding at 30 kph until your breathing returns to normal. Begin by warming up for 10 km at 25 kph. Then do the following work periods with appropriate rest in between: 1,500 meters, 1,400 meters, 1,300 meters, 1,200 meters, 1,100 meters, 1,000 meters, 900 meters, 800 meters, 700 meters, 600 meters, 500 meters, 400 meters, 300 meters, 200 meters. Finish with 10 km of easy pedaling. (Juniors and those not in top shape should start at 1,000 meters.) The reason for the progressively shorter work periods is to keep speed at maximum.

Here's another speed workout that can be done once or twice a week to improve the lactic acid system. The length of the rest periods will vary from individual to individual, but speed should stay at about 30 kph. Begin with a 5-10 km warm-up. Then do 2×4 km with 10-minute rests; 3×2 km with 4-minute rests; 4×1 km with 2-minute rests; 10×500 meters with 90-second rests. Finish with a 5-10 km cooldown.

There are several ways to improve your acceleration or jump. One way is to have a coach or friend in a car or on a motorcycle follow you and four or five others. Cruising speed should be 30-35 kph. When the coach gives the signal (honks the horn) the riders jump and ride at maximum speed. When the coach honks again the jump is over. The group reassembles and continues at 30 kph until the next signal. Several jumps can be done each session.

In another method, 10 riders carefully form a single line and move along at a brisk pace. The last rider pulls out and sprints to get to the front, easing up in time to avoid going too far ahead. Every rider must clearly understand that the pace of the group must be maintained, not increased. It must be possible for the last rider to reach the front with his sprint. Should he misjudge and go beyond the front rider, the latter should resist the temptation to increase speed to close the gap. Instead, he should carefully hold the pace and allow the gap to close gradually. This workout provides jump training, pace judgment, and tolerance to the bursts of maximal effort so often demanded in road and criterium racing.

Train efficiently with a heart rate monitor

One way to precisely measure your workouts is to use an electronic heart rate monitor.

The concept of training with a heart monitor has been around for several years, but it's only since Tony Rominger used it to prepare for his world hour record ride that the method has been widely accepted by cycling coaches. The recent introduction of moderately priced heart rate monitors has made such training practical for all cyclists.

A rapid pulse — anything above 160 bpm — is difficult to determine by hand. If you miss only 1 beat during a 10-second interval, your computed pulse would be off by 6 bpm. Accuracy in pulse ranges is important, yet a manually obtained pulse of 180 bpm may hide a true heart rate of 174 or 186.

Monitors provide accurate heart rates under the stress of hard cycling, so they can help you train efficiently in your safe heart rate target zone. Some units also have a high-low alarm function that warns you when you're outside of your desired range. For example, if you're trying to train at your anaerobic threshold, which may be 165 beats per minute, you can set the range at 162-168 bpm.

In addition to its accuracy, the monitor can serve as a source of biofeedback. Instantaneous and accurate monitoring allows you to adjust workout intensity to accommodate your body's response to such things as wind, terrain, and heat. Feedback allows you to adjust every exercise intensity to get the most out of each workout.

The most critical feature of a heart rate monitor is its method of pulse detection. The least expensive and least accurate method uses photo-reflectance to determine heart rate. Attached to a fingertip or earlobe, this kind of monitor uses a sensing photo cell and a light source. As the blood moves through the capillaries, the light passes from the light source to the photo cell. The resulting rhythmic changes in the pulse are sensed and then recorded by the monitor. Because monitors of this type are sensitive to body movements and so are easily skewed, they are generally not good for cycling.

Most of the more costly heart rate monitors read the electrical activity of the heart, much like an electrocardiogram. They are the most accurate and least affected by movement during cycling. Since the heart's electrical activity is transmitted through the skin, these models use a chest strap with rubber or adhesive electrodes. There are many models to choose from, including POLAR CIC, Cardio Sports, and Freestyle. Many cyclists prefer the wireless chest-strap units that transmit the pulse to a wristwatch receiver. Others like the kind that uses a wire to transmit data from the chest unit to a display unit on the wrist.

In addition to the high-low alarms, some models come with stopwatch capabilities to let you monitor both exercise time and recovery time. A nice feature included with some units is a memory capacity that can store your pulse at specific intervals so you can play it back after your workout.

Some units use an advanced radio-wave system that transmits your heart rate data to a receiver that can be attached to your wrist or slipped into a harness holder on the bicycle handlebars. These units do more than monitor your heart rate.

They are microcomputers that serve as multifunctional, pro-grammable training aids. They have an upper- and lower-limit alarm, a stopwatch, and a memory mode that records your heart rate at 30-second intervals throughout the workout so it can be played back later. Some even come with a computer interface. The information can be sent from the watch to the printer to give you a graphic printout of your workout heart rate.

The relationship between the features in pulse monitors and their price is — not surprisingly — linear. You can expect to pay as little as $100 for the crudest monitor and as much as $400 for the most sophisticated. If you want accurate information, spend the money on a reliable unit.

Peaking must be planned

When successful cyclists are able to be in top form for the big events, we say they have peaked. Though many cyclists have heard the term, few know how to go about peaking.

Peaking for a race doesn't just happen. It requires months, even years, of preparation. Five-time Tour de France winner Bernard Hinault, for example, established interim goals for four years before entering and winning his first Tour de France.

Peaking requires setting goals for yourself and having the self-discipline to achieve those goals. In fact, having a goal to work toward makes self-discipline and setting priorities easier. That goal may be to break an hour for the 40 km time trial or to win a major road race. You should establish your goals early in the season and they should be based on past performance, physical capabilities, and input from a coach when possible. Goals are not absolute and may be adjusted as training pro-gresses.

Peaking consists of a gradual build-up of distance and effort, with a final phase of training to work on speed and technique.

During the final rest or taper period, the body is recharged with energy and psychologically you are hungry to compete at your best.

Peaking is often difficult to plan for because of the crowded race schedule and the variety of races offered. It's one thing to peak for a specific event, another to peak for a series of races. Throw in the district championships, national championships, and world championships, and you can begin to appreciate the difficulty of scheduling peaks. Sometimes you must choose to train through certain events in order to prepare for your goal races.

Most athletes, coaches, and exercise scientists say you can only peak two, or at most three times per year. (Track cyclists and criterium specialists can peak more often, because shorter events take less toll on the body.) You'll need a minimum of six to eight weeks between goal events in order to perform well. For example, you may peak for a late spring stage race and then again for the nationals in late summer. Between the two events you still need to rebuild for at least a month, doing one-day events and gradually working up to short stage races.

During the 10-14 days before the event you should cut down on distance work and add speed and last-minute technique training to your program. All hard training should end five to seven days before the event and be replaced with easy riding each day, with a few jumps when you feel good.

Successful peaking depends on consistent training, so have a program that plans for the whole year. Be sure to rest sufficiently after all races to fully restore your energy and avoid riding when you're sick. And don't do anything foolish in training or racing that could lead to a crash. You don't want to lose training time because of injuries.

Remember that while the annals of cycling are filled with stories of outstanding riders who succeeded at the big events, there are many others who lined up as leading contenders but failed. It should have been their moment but they weren't prepared to seize it because, in many cases, they hadn't properly peaked for the competition. The secret to success in road or track cycling is being prepared for top performance at the right time.

Mental training can provide an edge

Although many sports feature psychological training as a major part of their program, cycling has been slow to follow. Yet there is little doubt that elite cyclists succeed because of psychological as well as physiological capabilities. As riders reach the top levels of competition, their mental training becomes more and more important. The cyclist who can best control psychological energy will have the decisive edge.

Mental techniques for improving performance are not new. The Soviets and East Germans have for years offered intensive psychological training to their top athletes. Other countries are now following suit and many have their own traveling team psychologists.

One major concern for many athletes is managing stress, particularly before a big event. A technique developed by Dr. Richard Suinn of Colorado State University involves the use of relaxation and imagery to strengthen mental and motor skills. Dr. Suinn has worked with U.S. alpine, cross-country, and modern pentathlon team members. Dr. Andrew Jacobs, who works with U.S. Olympic cyclists, has also used this technique.

The technique begins with a 20-minute period of isometric-like tensing and relaxing of the muscle groups, which is then followed by the imagery session.

The tensing/relaxing stage works as follows:

1. Find a quiet place to lie down. Close your eyes and try to become as relaxed as possible.
2. Make both hands into fists and become aware of how this tenseness feels.
3. Relax both hands and focus on the feeling of relaxation.
4. Repeat steps 2 and 3 with the following muscle groups:
   — Forehead: frown hard and relax.
   — Eyes: close tightly and relax with them still closed.
   — Facial muscles: clench jaws and relax.
   — Chest: take a deep breath and hold until you feel tension, then exhale and relax.
   — Biceps: bend arms at elbow, contract muscles, then relax.
   — Thighs: contract and relax.
   — Lower legs and feet: point toes downward and relax.
5. Follow this with a deep breath and feel your whole body beginning to unwind. Repeat steps 2-4 two more times.

Immediately following the relaxation phase, begin the imagery process:

1. Remaining quiet, take the first pleasant thought that comes to mind and build upon it. Use it to become more relaxed and dwell upon it for 10-15 seconds.
2. Repeat with one or two other thoughts.
3. Select an element of the event you're preparing for or wish to practice. It may be the initial acceleration of the kilometer, the pull at the front in a team time trial — whatever. Remain relaxed. Switch on the scene. (For

example, imagine the scene just before the start command of the kilometer.) Breathe deeply, retain the scene, and continue to let the body relax.

4. Practice in your mind the skill you wish to execute to precision. Feel the motions as if everything was exactly right and this was a gold-medal ride.
5. Make sure to complete the entire skill before you stop.
6. Use short scenes until your imagery technique develops. Then gradually lengthen them as long as you can remain calm and in charge of the process.

When practiced regularly, this technique can reduce pre-race stress and can actually improve your performance. The imagery technique can also be used to help you perform well in poor environmental conditions (such as bad roads, rain, or gusting wind), and during recovery from injury. For example, a cyclist who has been badly injured may hold back when he returns to the bike. Imagery can be used to eliminate this unintentional protective reaction while reinforcing skill.

The relaxation-and-imagery technique is only one example of how sports psychology is being used. The future promises new methods to help athletes achieve the most from their minds and bodies.

6 / Off-season training

Tour de France winner Jan Ulrich has used cross-country skiing in the winter as part of his off season training program. Ruthie Matthes and John Tomac are other top U.S. pros who regularly include cross-country skiing, hiking, and mountain biking in their winter programs.

These three riders are not alone in choosing to pursue alternative exercise during the off-season. Many cyclists turn to other aerobic activities during the winter to maintain physical fitness. Some do so because it's too cold and icy to ride a bike, others because they simply need a psychological change.

Every other day is enough

Surprisingly, you don't have to work out vigorously every day to maintain optimal function of the heart, lungs, and circulatory system. To maintain aerobic fitness, you need to exercise four or five days a week for 30-60 minutes. Working out every other day is usually sufficient, particularly if you're doing exercises like running and weight lifting, which are more stressful than cycling to the musculo-skeletal system. You need to allow enough time between workouts for your body to recover from the unaccustomed stress.

The level of training intensity you can tolerate will vary depending on your fitness, general health, age, and ability to perform the activity you choose. Recent research indicates a heart rate of 75% of maximum will produce a training effect. If you haven't had your maximal heart rate determined through testing, you can estimate it by subtracting your age from 220.

In my experiences with young adult cyclists, I've found that a training heart rate in the range of 150-170 beats per minute provides adequate stimulation to the heart and circulatory system. For riders over 35, because of the decline in maximal heart rate due to aging, a rate of 130-140 beats is probably adequate.

Running

One popular winter exercise is running. Regardless of what some people believe, running is not detrimental to cyclists. In fact, several national team riders use running as part of their off-season conditioning programs.

If you decide to run, be sure to begin each session with a warm-up and finish with a cool-down. A 10-minute warm-up period should include slow running or jogging, push-ups, and flexibility exercises. The cool-down should allow adequate time for various body functions to readjust to normal. The length of the cool-down depends on the difficulty of the exercise session and on the environmental conditions. It will normally last from 5-10 minutes and include such activities as jogging, walking, and stretching.

Even if you're a national class cyclist, you'll discover that running uses different sets of muscles in different ways, so expect muscle soreness at first. This soreness shouldn't be so uncomfortable that you can't keep running. If it is, you're overdoing it and should reduce both distance and speed until the soreness subsides.

Keep injuries to a minimum by wearing shoes specifically designed for running and by incorporating a stretching regimen into your routine. Stretching before and after every run will provide the most benefit, but if that's not possible, do at least one stretching session daily. There's no denying that running tightens the leg muscles, particularly the hamstrings. Regular stretching helps develop the necessary flexibility in your muscles, ligaments, and tendons to enable you to run comfortably and remain injury-free.

The key to a successful running program is to go at your own pace, using your heart rate as the indicator of stress, and to keep the intensity of your running sessions well within your limits.

If you have trouble running continuously for 30-60 minutes, try mixing in some walking. Alternate running periods of 300-500 meters with 50-meter walks. The walking segments are important because they represent a semi-recovery period. This way you never reach the exhaustion point, and you're less likely to develop muscle soreness. Gradually cut back on the walking while increasing the amount of running. Once you're able to run for 10 minutes or cover a mile without stopping, you can eliminate the walking intervals entirely.

Hiking

If you want to keep exercising outdoors in the winter and you have access to challenging terrain, consider adding hiking to your program once or twice a week. Hiking is one exercise that has practically no disadvantages.

Hiking a few hours a day is comparable to a ride of several hours. The uphills provide the best aerobic exercise. Thigh muscles get an excellent workout and if the pace is fast enough or enough altitude is gained your cardiovascular system is adequately stressed. Take the downhills with caution, though, and keep the straining and holding back to a minimum. Be careful of foot placement and don't overextend your stride.

It's okay to hike alone if the territory is familiar, but if you're going into unknown areas or on an extended day trip, hike with a group for safety. Always take along a pack with food and extra clothes. For an additional workout, add some weight to the pack.

An excellent book on hiking is *Mountaineering: The Freedom of the Hills*. Seattle: Mountaineers, 1997.

Cross-country skiing

If you happen to live in an area where snow is plentiful during the winter, cross-country skiing using either the diagonal stride or skating technique (or a combination) can provide an excellent physical challenge. It requires great endurance, strength, power, speed, and coordination — all the things a cyclist should develop in the off-season.

Lightweight skiing equipment is readily available at a modest cost. And with the advent of telemark technology, you no longer have to be restricted to the tracks of the local cross-country touring center. Metal-edge skis, improved bindings, and shoes with more lateral support have brought this sport out of the track and into the backcountry.

Several books on skiing are available, including:

— Sharkey, Brian. *Training for Cross-country Ski Racing.*
— Gillette, Ned and John Dostal. *Cross Country Skiing.*
— Mansfield, Dick. *Skating on Skis.*

Snowshoeing

Name an outdoor winter exercise that doesn't require lessons or a heavy financial investment. Snowshoeing fits that description.

If snowshoeing brings to mind images of a lonely trapper plowing through the endless wastes of the frozen north, you're in for a surprise. Recreational snowshoeing is a fast-growing, economical sport that liberates the outdoor winter enthusiast from the narrow confines of cities and surfaced roads. A pair of snowshoes turns deep winter drifts into pathways to back-woods scenery. In many areas where there is abundant brush, rocky terrain, or thick woods, snowshoes will outperform skis. Even athletes who run regularly are finding snowshoeing a more satisfying alternative, and one that's just as aerobic.

Today's "Western-style" snowshoe features a metal frame and solid decking. This construction is a radical departure from the traditional wood-and-gut design and makes the shoes more durable. Several endurance athletes in Colorado are now using a snowshoe called Redfeather that lets them run with speed and power. The shoes are manufactured by Redfeather, which is based in Leadville, Colorado.

Like any sport, snowshoeing is more enjoyable when you understand the fundamentals. One complete how-to book is: Prater, Gene. *Snowshoeing*. Seattle: Mountaineers, 1988.

Rollerblade skating

Rollerblades may best be described as "in-line" roller skates. The wheels are aligned one behind the other instead of side-by-side as on conventional roller skates. This alignment results in an altogether different sensation and easier maneuverability. Rollerblades are designed for outdoor use on paved or cement surfaces — the smoother the surface, the better the skates will perform.

Rollerblading provides a good cardiovascular workout. It also exercises the same leg muscles as cycling does and is better than running for riders with ankle and knee problems because it eliminates impact stress. It also works your upper body since you move your arms right along with your legs to maintain momentum. Some athletes use ski poles to help propel themselves forward.

Take your workouts indoors

There will be times when you can't or don't want to exercise outdoors. Maybe the mercury has dropped into the danger zone or you've simply run out of daylight hours. In such cases, take your workout indoors.

Probably the most useful indoor exercise for the cyclist is pedaling on a bicycle ergometer or windload trainer. An ergometer is a stationary device used primarily in physiological testing to measure work output. The frame is solidly constructed and the cranks turn a heavy wheel located in front of the rider. With windload trainers, you mount your own bike on a weighted flywheel device. Turned by your bike's rear wheel, the flywheel draws in air and disperses it radially. The acceleration of air mass creates a torque that increases exponentially with speed, just like wind on the road.

Because they effectively simulate real road riding, ergometers and windload simulators can help you develop many of the specific characteristics needed for cycling. They can also be used to evaluate your fitness during the season. The idea is to do an identical workout each time and check your heart rate at the end. When it is lower than before, you know your training program is working.

Almost any type of training done on the road can be simulated on an ergometer or windload trainer, including intervals, sprints, power work, and endurance training. Training on an ergometer or windload trainer is exhausting, so be careful not to overdo it. Many a naive cyclist has worked into a state of fatigue by not following a progressive and organized program. Be sure to allow adequate rest between repetitions and workouts. Warm up properly before every training session and follow each workout with a cool-down period.

Rowing

Rowing works the major muscle groups and provides excellent aerobic conditioning, all with less joint stress than running and other impact exercises.

Rowing machines come in a wide variety of models and prices, ranging from low-tech versions that sell for less than $100 to the video-game-like Liferower, which sells for more than $2,700. A current favorite among many indoor rowers is the Concept II ergometer, which features an electronic performance monitor that provides information about distance rowed, calories consumed, stroke rate, and elapsed time.

An excellent aerobic exercise, rowing benefits the heart, lungs, and circulatory system as you work the muscles of your legs, back, shoulders, buttocks, arms, and stomach. (Those stronger back and shoulder muscles will help you be a better climber and time trialist on the bike.) Beginners should remember, though, that since rowing works all the major muscle groups, they will probably tire quickly.

Even, easy strokes are the key to completing a workout. Aim for 22-24 strokes per minute. Only after you can comfortably row for 20 minutes should you add some power workouts to your program. You can accomplish this by increasing resistance and stroke speed.

Stair climbing

Although many people complain about how many flights of stairs they have to climb in a day, some cyclists have actually begun to brag about it. Stair climbing is excellent exercise. In addition to its aerobic benefits, it provides conditioning for a variety of muscles, including the hamstrings, buttocks, and — especially — the quadriceps.

If you don't live in a city with buildings over 25 stories tall, you may be able to find a stair-climbing simulator at your local fitness club. Such simulators aren't as ubiquitous as cycling or rowing ergometers, but they're becoming more common.

Two major brands are currently on the market, and both will give you an excellent workout.

For those determined to tax their bodies to the limit, the Vesa Climber should do the trick. You may remember this ladder-like ergometer from the movie *Rocky IV* — it was one of the Soviet fighter's high-tech training aids. It incorporates moving hand and foot grips to produce a climbing motion that pumps, pulls, and pushes virtually every muscle of your body from the neck down. With a step height that can be varied from 1 to 20 inches, a wide selection of speeds, and 15 programmable work levels, this machine is capable of taxing even the fittest of athletes.

Another machine, the StairMaster 6000 ergometer, is best described as a small "down" escalator that you walk up. Equipped with a computer into which you program your age, weight, and the number of flights you plan to climb, it calculates caloric expenditure, power output, rate of exercise, and duration. Climbing speed can be adjusted from 45 to 115 steps per minute.

Another model, the StairMaster 4000 PT, uses left and right footrests that rise and drop with every step you take. Since your feet never leave the footrests, exercising on these units is relatively trauma-free. Workloads on the 4000 can't be set as high as on the 6000.

Ski simulators

Indoor cross-country skiing machines are as effective as bicycle and rowing ergometers when it comes to conditioning, and they also develop upper-body strength — something most cyclists can use. Recently, while recovering from a knee injury, I had the chance to try out a NordicTrack Pro, one of the better-known indoor ski machines. It provided an excellent workout for both upper and lower body.

You don't have to be an experienced skier to use a ski simulator. Your feet are secured to the skis, which rest on rollers. A pad keeps you from falling forward as your arms pull back and forth on cables, simulating the push and pull of ski poles. A flywheel regulates the tension appropriately, so you can glide through a workout. Though the movement might feel awkward at first, within one or two workouts you should feel comfortable and be able to start concentrating on improving your technique.

Beware of windchill

During February and March it's tempting to stay in the warmth of the house and ride your windload trainer, but as the racing season approaches it becomes necessary to begin riding regularly outside. Sometimes this can be a problem, since extreme cold is a health hazard.

When is it safe to go out and when should you keep your workout indoors? Your first consideration should be to determine the effective windchill temperature by using the chart in this chapter. A rider who tries to train when there is "great danger" is only asking for trouble. "Increasing danger" means that special care should be used in dressing. "Little danger" signifies just that.

Wind direction is an important factor. Wind from the side or behind has only a fraction of the impact of a headwind. Speed is also a consideration; the faster you ride into the wind, the more the windchill is increased. Whenever possible, begin your ride against the wind so that the second half will find it

WINDCHILL TEMPERATURE

Wind speed (mph)	Air temperature (degrees Fahrenheit)							
	+50	+40	+30	+20	+10	0	−10	−20
5	48	37	27	16	6	−5	−15	−26
10	40	28	16	4	−9	−24	−33	−46
15	36	22	9	−5	−18	−32	−45	−58
20	32	18	4	−10	−25	−39	−53	−67
25	30	16	0	−15	−29	−44	−59	−74
30	28	13	−2	−18	−33	−48	−63	−79
35	27	11	−4	−20	−35	−51	−67	−82
40	26	10	−6	−21	−37	−53	−69	−85

| LITTLE DANGER | INCREASING DANGER | GREAT DANGER |

The stronger the wind, the lower the effective air temperature. Cyclists need to be especially careful in cold weather because their rate of travel can increase the windchill factor.

at your back. This way perspiration won't be as dangerous or uncomfortable when skin temperature begins to drop. On very cold days it may be safest to break training into two parts, if your schedule permits. Do half the day's mileage in mid morning and the remainder in mid afternoon.

To judge wind speed, look at the trees. At 20 mph, small branches move and dust or snow is raised. At 30 mph, large branches move. At 40, whole trees move. (You can just feel a 10-mph wind lightly on your face.)

There has never been a documented case of lungs being frozen by frigid air, but the danger of frostbite is real to other areas, and frostbite should not be taken lightly since it can disable or kill. Your ears, cheeks, nose, fingers, and toes are most susceptible. The signs are tingling and redness followed by paleness and numbness. If you suspect frostbite, don't walk on or massage the frozen parts. Place them in water that is about body temperature and seek medical help immediately.

Cold-weather clothing should protect and insulate all skin surfaces. It works better to wear several light to moderate layers of synthetic wicking material shirts and a breathable wind breaker. (For more on winter-worthy clothing, see chapter 15.)

When there is no wind, dress for the cold. When the wind is blowing, wear something that will keep it out. Wear clothing that allows you to maintain normal body temperature in a wide range of conditions. A long-sleeved, zipper-front jacket with attached hood is very versatile. When the wind is howling in your face, you can zip the front and use the hood under your helmet. If you begin to get hot, you can make two adjustments (zipper and hood) that will allow you to release the heat build-up.

Never ride in winter without a hat because heat is lost rapidly through the head and neck. (A pullover ski mask gives good protection on frigid days.) Mittens will keep your hands warmer than gloves because they merge the heat of the hands and the fingers. Feet are always a problem, but layering will help there, too. Put on wool knee-length ski socks, then the shoes, then an old stretched pair of thick wool socks with holes cut out for the cleats. Over everything, zip on cycling booties.

A useful acronym to remember during winter is VIP: ventilate, insulate, and protect. Ventilate excess perspiration. Insulate, particularly high-blood-flow areas like the neck and head. Protect from wind and wetness with appropriate clothing.

Even with the best of precautions, however, hypothermia may occur. Hypothermia arises when the core temperature of the body is lowered. It can happen when exposure and exhaustion cause the body to lose more heat than it can produce and so normal body temperature can no longer be maintained. You can develop hypothermia in temperatures well above freezing if the right combination of cold, wet, and wind is present.

If you begin to shiver on a ride, either work harder until the shivering stops or go home. Dry yourself and change into dry clothes as soon as possible. Then cover yourself with warm blankets. Take in hot liquids and warm foods, especially carbohydrates. If the shivering does not subside, contact a physician immediately.

You'll be bothered more by the cold during the first few days of training than you will after a few weeks, because your body will begin to acclimatize. You'll begin producing more heat. Research has shown that after six weeks of exercising in the cold, exposing fingers to the cold for four hours results in less temperature drop, less numbness, and less reduction in blood flow than occurred before the start of acclimatization.

The hardest part of winter cycling may simply be getting started. Conditions outside often look colder than they really are. In most cases you'll find that riding is quite comfortable once you get underway.

7 / Strength training

Until the late 1980's, many U.S. coaches and riders believed that strength training would only add excess body weight and inhibit the smooth, supple pedal motion a cyclists needs to spin at 90 rpm or more.

But attitudes have changed. Most experts now contend that proper strength training will help any athlete, male or female, young or old. The stronger the athlete is, the more likely he will be to reap the benefits of greater speed, flexibility, endurance, and resistance to injury.

Of course, some world-class cyclists say they've never used strength training. Does that mean you don't need it? Think about it. Almost all outstanding riders are blessed with superior neurological and physiological systems. Add to this training, skill, and race experience, and it's no wonder their performance level is far above average, even when their strength and power may not be. Imagine how well they would do if their bodies were truly strong.

Increase strength to get more endurance

I believe a strength program is mandatory if you're to reach your full potential as a cyclist. But before you begin setting up a program, it's important to have an understanding of power and strength and their relationship.

Strength is the maximal force that a muscle or muscle group can exert in one contraction. It's easy to see how important strength is for the weight lifter or shot putter, but what benefit does it have for the cyclist, whose muscles must contract again and again, thousands of times? Research has shown that muscular endurance is significantly related to maximum strength. If a cyclist succeeds in making his muscles stronger, he will also increase their endurance. Even short events like the 1,000-meter time trial, individual pursuit, and match sprint require muscular endurance. And imagine how much a rider's start or jump could be improved by increasing muscular strength.

Power is calculated by multiplying force by distance then dividing by time. Force is the work put into the pedals; distance is the length of the race; time is the duration of the event. You can increase power by exerting more force on the pedals or by pedaling faster in the same gear. Increasing muscular strength is one way to increase force and power in cycling.

The experience of athletes in other sports has taught us the value of a specific strength training program. That is, the best weight exercises are those that work the muscles relevant to the sport, or the muscles that become weak and imbalanced because they aren't used at all. For cycling, all the major muscle groups need to be strengthened.

There are four basic weight training methods:

— Isotonic exercise, in which the muscle contracts with varying tension while lifting a constant load.
— Isometric exercise, in which tension develops but there is no change in the length of the muscle.
— Isokinetic exercise, in which the speed of contraction is fixed and there is maximum muscular tension during the full range of motion.

— Accommodating-resistance exercise, in which the resistance varies during an isotonic movement. This is done with machines such as Nautilus and Universal.

ADVANTAGES AND DISADVANTAGES OF WEIGHT TRAINING DEVICES

Equipment	Contraction	Advantages	Disadvantages
Free weights	Isotonic	— Equipment is inexpensive — Equipment is generally available — Specific exercises may be designed	— Workout time is increased with changing weight
Immovable resistance device	Isometric	— Little time involved — Minimal equipment	— Boring — Hard to record progress — Specificity of cycling movement hard to produce
Universal	Accommodating resistance	— Lever system that allows the resistance to change to match the joint's ability to produce a force — Psychologically rewarding	— Expensive — Cannot accurately record weight lifted
Nautilus	Accommodating resistance	— Cam System — See "Universal" remarks	— Expensive — Plates lifted do not accurately tell force applied
Cybex	Isokinetic	— Exercise can be carried out with maximum resistance throughout the full range of the muscle — Speed can be slow to fast	— Expensive — Exercise movements are limited
Mini-Gym Exer-Geni	Isokinetic	— Inexpensive — Can adapt equipment to specific exercises	— Hard to evaluate progress

---

Weight training develops strength, which improves endurance in cycling. What method you use will depend on the equipment available.

The training method you use is often determined by the equipment available. The table lists the advantages and disadvantages of various training devices. Note that true isokinetic equipment (Cybex) is not readily available and does not provide a comprehensive training program because of the limited number of movements it allows.

Progressive resistance builds power

A strength training program should be based on progressive resistance, or in other words, adding weight over time as your strength increases. Begin by determining the most weight you can lift one time. This is done by experimentation, adding more weight and attempting one-lift repetitions for each exercise. Do three sets of six repetitions for each exercise. The first set is done with 85% of maximum; the second with 80% of maximum; the third with 75% of maximum. (Before attempting maximum lifts, be sure to warm up well, and have someone with you for safety.)

For example, in the bench press, let's say you can manage 1 rep with 150 pounds. Your 3 sets would be 6 reps with 125 pounds, 6 reps with 120 lbs, 6 reps with 115 pounds. This schedule will allow you to stress your muscles to the limit throughout the three sets. After three or four weeks, test your maximum lifts again and adjust the workout weights accordingly.

The next table lists the major muscle groups and the exercises that strengthen them using Nautilus, Universal, and free weights. All three methods work well as long as you follow the principle of progressive resistance and use proper technique. Correct technique is also extremely important for your safety. Ask the instructor at the health club or gym for advice and read the appropriate training manual.

MUSCLE GROUPS AND EXERCISE METHODS

Muscles exercised	Free weights	Nautilus equipment	Universal equipment
Forearm	Wrist curl	Multi-exercise	Wrist curl
Biceps	Standing curl	Biceps curl Compound curl Chin-up	Chin-up Curl
Triceps	Reverse curl	Triceps extension Compound extension Parallel dip	Reverse curl Parallel dip
Lower back, butocks	Deadlifts squat	Leg press Squat Hip and back	Leg press
Quadriceps	Squat	Squat Leg press Leg extension	Leg press Leg extension
Hamstrings	Squat	Squat Leg press Leg curl	Leg press Leg curl
Calves	Calf raise	Calf raise Toe press	Toe press on leg press
Stomach	Sit-up	Adominal Leg raise and side bend on multi-exercise	Sit-up Leg raise
Latissimus dorsi	Bent-over rowing	Torso/arm Chin-up Pullover	Chin-up Pulldown on lat machine
Deltoids	Military press Behind neck press Upright rowing	Omni shoulder Double shoulder	Seated press Upright rowing
Trapezius	Shoulder shrug	Neck and shoulder	Shoulder shrug
Pectoralis	Bench press	Double chest Omni shoulder	Bench press Parallel dip

Athletes need to develop the muscles used in their sport and also the muscles that become weak because they aren't used as much. For cycling, all the major muscle groups usually need to be strengthened.

What is the best time of year for strength training and how frequently should workouts be done? Generally, cyclists should do their weight work in the winter and during preseason training. Start with workouts twice per week, working up to a maximum of three times per week.

Strength and endurance seem to subside at slower rates than they develop. A study showed that all the strength gained during a three-week isotonic training program was not lost during the following six weeks of no training. Second, strength was maintained or slightly improved during a subsequent six-week program that consisted of just one set of one repetition done with maximum weight.

This emphasizes that the most difficult phase of a resistance training program is the development of strength and endurance. To then maintain strength, exercises need only be done once a week or once every two weeks. For cyclists, this means that one upper-body session per week throughout the season should do it.

A strength training program may enable you to develop and hold an edge over your competitors, even those who seem blessed with more natural ability on the bike. Start your strength training in December so you'll be at your physical peak by the time the important races arrive.

Circuit training improves total conditioning

In the last few years, circuit training has become a popular method of increasing strength and total body conditioning. Circuit training is a sport-specific, well-designed arrangement of exercises. You perform specific exercises at various stations, usually within a limited period of time. At the conclusion of one exercise you move rapidly to the next station. Once you've done the exercises in all the stations, the circuit is complete.

The exercises usually involve weight lifting, but running, stationary cycling, calisthenics, and stretching may also be included. Circuit training can be designed to increase muscular strength, endurance, flexibility, and cardiovascular fitness.

The circuit should include exercises that develop your total body fitness, with emphasis on the muscle groups used in cycling. There are usually between 10 and 15 stations, one circuit of which requires 10-20 minutes to complete. You perform several circuits during the workout, with 15 seconds of rest between stations.

At resistance stations, the weights should be such that your muscles are fatigued after performing as many repetitions as possible within a designated time period (for example, 30 seconds). Add more weight when you notice a significant rise in the number of repetitions. Arrange the stations so the same muscle group is not being exercised at consecutive stations.

Here's an example of a circuit for cyclists. You may not be able to set up an identical circuit, so be innovative and set up a program with whatever resources you have available.

Station	Exercise
1	Bicycle ergometer or windload trainer (3 min)
2	Bent-knee sit-ups
3	Bent-over rowing
4	Dead lift
5	Leg press
6	Arm curl
7	Bicycle ergometer
8	Upright rowing
9	Leg curl (knee flexion)
10	Bench press
11	Back hyperextension
12	Calf raises

Circuits per session: 2-3
Weight load: 40-55% of 1 maximum repetition
Repetitions: As many as possible in 30 seconds
Rest: 15 seconds between stations
Frequency: 2-3 sessions per week

For more information on these and other weight training exercises, see: Pearl, Bill & Moran, Gary. *Getting Stronger*. Shelter Publications, 1995; or Burke, Edmund. *Off-Season Training for Cyclists*, Velo, 1997.

A circuit using Universal Gym-type equipment is excellent because you can change the weight quickly. However, you don't need expensive equipment. You can set up a circuit in your basement or garage with whatever you have at hand. For example, if you don't have an ergometer or windload trainer, substitute a 440- or 660-yard run.

Jump for strength with plyometrics

Another strength training program that many cyclists use is called plyometrics. Plyometrics, simply defined, is a series of drills that places muscles in a stretched position before they shorten (concentric contraction). The results are said to be improved strength, speed, and explosive power.

Plyometric training overloads the muscles via jumping movements. When you land from a jump (see illustration), the muscles tense while lengthening to a stretched position (eccentric contraction). This is followed immediately by an explosive concentric contraction (another jump). The goal is to simulate the movements and speed of contraction used in competition.

If you have difficulty visualizing this, think of a rubber band and how it responds to stretch. When you increase the stretch, the tension and the speed of shortening of the rubber band become greater.

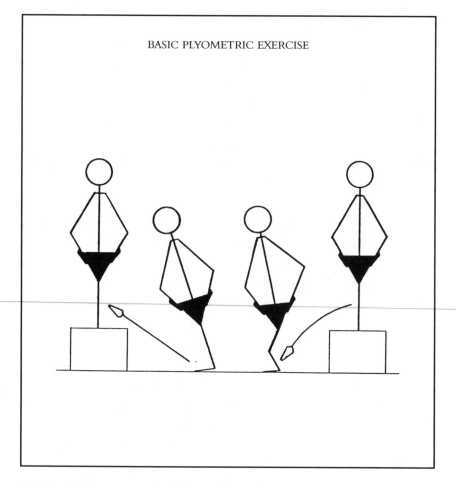

BASIC PLYOMETRIC EXERCISE

The jumping movements of plyometric training help improve the muscles' stretching and contracting abilities, increasing strength and power.

Muscle has contracting and elastic components, both involved in the development of force. When the elastic component is stretched, tension is produced. Muscles also have stretch receptors. Invoking the stretch reflex of a muscle in combination with a voluntary contraction results in a more vigorous contraction. In plyometrics, a muscle's elastic component and stretch reflex contribute to the total force generated in a contraction.

Research has shown that plyometrics increases strength and power. In a study with collegiate football players, one group used plyometric drills (jumping from a height of 45 cm) in combination with weight training. A control group did only conventional weight training exercises. After six weeks the group using plyometrics had greater gains in strength.

In another study, subjects used a jumping height of 34 inches and gradually added weight (with a weight vest) up to 20 pounds. After 8 weeks there was an increase of more than 2 inches in vertical jump, a 10% improvement.

Plyometrics can be used like weight training, applying the overload principle by progressively increasing the number of repetitions, the number of sets, the height of the jumping block, and the weight in the weight vest. As with any training program, the athlete's age must be considered. A mature cyclist can usually handle rigorous workouts. A Senior can probably use plyometrics year-round, while a Junior should use it only in the off-season.

You should be careful not to overload the thigh muscles, which may lead to knee pain. Use progressive resistance and don't overstrain your muscles.

Plyometrics is best suited to cyclists who need to develop power, speed, and acceleration. Those who compete in the kilometer, match sprint, pursuit, and 100-km team time trial can expect significant improvement from a progressive plyometric program. The long-distance road specialist may wish to use it only in the off-season.

The diagram shows various plyometric exercises suitable for cyclists. During the first three weeks, limit your workout to broad jumps, triple jumps, single-leg hops, and jumps off low boxes. Work out twice a week, doing no more than 60 jumping movements (repetitions) per session.

After three weeks, increase the sessions to every other day and the repetitions to 75-85. Incorporate a variety of hopping

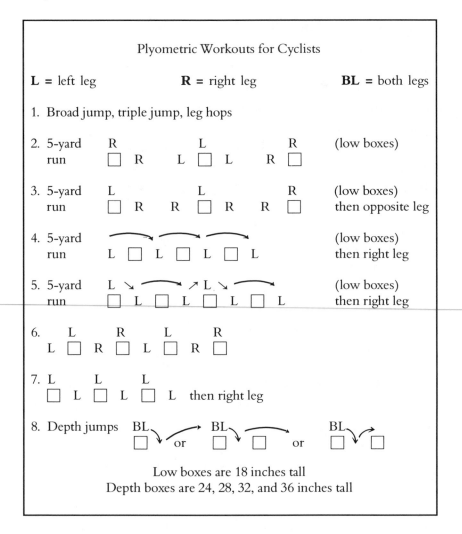

Plyometric Workouts for Cyclists

L = left leg   **R** = right leg   **BL** = both legs

1. Broad jump, triple jump, leg hops

2. 5-yard run   R   □ R   L   L □   L   R   R □   (low boxes)

3. 5-yard run   L   □ R   R   L □   R   R   R □   (low boxes) then opposite leg

4. 5-yard run   L   □ L   □ L   □ L   (low boxes) then right leg

5. 5-yard run   □ L   L □   L □   L □   L   (low boxes) then right leg

6. L   □ L   R   R □   L   L □   R   R □

7. L   □ L   L   □ L   L   □ L   then right leg

8. Depth jumps   BL □   or   BL □   □   or   BL □   □

Low boxes are 18 inches tall
Depth boxes are 24, 28, 32, and 36 inches tall

Road riders may want to do plyometric exercises only in the off-season, but track cyclists can probably benefit from them year-round. It will take several weeks to work up to a program like this one.

exercises into your program. For example, hop on your right leg, left, right, etc., as you would in exaggerated running. Or try right, right, left, left, or all right leg or all left. Do these hops for 30 yards at full speed. Add jumps from boxes 14-24 inches high. This phase should last about four weeks.

After a month you can increase the height of the boxes and wear a weight vest. Don't use ankle weights — they're too hard on the feet and ankles. Add bounding up stairs. The maximum number of repetitions per workout should be 100.

Keep your hands on your hips during all exercises. Using your arms is cheating and takes away from the work of the legs. Once the racing season arrives, you can continue to do one or two plyometric sessions per week, depending on your needs.

NUTRITION

8 / Fuel for endurance

Nutrition, like politics or religion, is a subject that inspires passionate convictions. Though many of these convictions are valid, I recommend that you be conservative in your choice of diet, and practice a common-sense approach.

Recent research suggests that the athlete's diet should be composed of at least 60% carbohydrates, 20-25% fats, and the rest proteins. This is quite a change from the 50-30-20 ratio widely recommended just a few years ago.

Athletes need extra carbohydrates

The greater amount of carbohydrates is necessary because carbohydrates are used to form glucose, the preferred fuel burned by muscles during exercise. Hard exercise depletes blood glucose and the glucose stored in the muscles (glycogen), which must be replaced before you can exercise at the same level again. Many athletes routinely fail to adequately replenish their glucose stores. This may explain the lethargy, staleness, and difficulty in recovery such athletes experience after a period of hard training.

Nutritionists divide carbohydrates into two categories — simple and complex. Simple carbohydrates are highly refined.

Examples include jam, candy, syrup, chocolate, and table sugar. Complex carbohydrates are found in unrefined foods such as peas, beans, pasta, potatoes, nuts, and whole grains like rice, oats, and barley. Since complex carbohydrates provide not only carbohydrates but vitamins, minerals, and fiber as well, they are nutritious and the best choice for your daily diet.

Researchers have found that the muscles' ability to form glycogen is greatest in the first few hours after exercise, so it's important to begin replacing carbohydrates as soon as possible after a hard workout. (Unfortunately, that's also usually the time when you feel least like eating!) Try to eat a total of 100-120 grams (the amount found in three ounces of oatmeal or 12 ounces of a carbohydrate replacement drink like Exceed High Carbohydrate Source or Gatorlode) immediately after exercise and again two hours later.

Studies also indicate that you can temporarily increase muscle glycogen stores with carbohydrate loading, a technique many athletes use for major events. Carbohydrate loading begins about a week before competition. On days one through three, carbohydrate should be about 50% of calorie intake, increasing to about 70% on days four through six, with competition on day seven. Training intensity should be gradually reduced during the week.

Because the glycogen stores are first depleted, the body supercompensates by storing larger amounts once carbohydrates become available. Research has shown that carbohydrate loading produces very high levels of muscle glycogen. Values of 4 grams per 100 grams of muscles have been recorded, as compared to the normal amount of 1.5 per 100 grams of muscle.

Is carbohydrate loading safe? The evidence is not conclusive. It has been linked to one case of cardiac arrythmia and some research indicates that high accumulation of muscle glycogen may be associated with a gain in water weight, blood in the urine, abnormal heart beat, and increased concentration of fat in the blood. Other studies, however, indicate that there are few, if any, negative side effects.

The best approach is to make a high-carbohydrate diet part of your daily regimen and to use the carbohydrate loading technique two or three times a year before major competitions.

Burn fat for energy

During hard efforts, your body relies almost exclusively on glucose for energy. But when the intensity of exercise is low enough, or when your glucose stores are depleted, your body will use fat for fuel.

Fat has the advantage of being present in the body in a nearly inexhaustible supply. The average cyclist has only 4,000 calories of carbohydrate reserves to draw on, whereas even the fittest athlete has at least 50,000 calories of fat to use for energy. Fat also provides more energy per gram, yielding 9 calories per gram as compared to 4 calories per gram of carbohydrate. And, if you can burn more fat, you'll be able to save your glycogen stores for when you need them — during those hard efforts.

The ability to burn fat appears to be related to the ability to consume oxygen (max VO_2). At a given workload, a cyclist with a lower max VO_2 will produce more lactic acid because he is working more anaerobically than a cyclist with a higher max VO_2. (See chapter 2.) High levels of lactic acid in the blood may interfere with the release of free fatty acids (the form in which fat is metabolized for energy). Also, trained muscle has a greater capacity to use free fatty acids than untrained muscle. This, plus the increased ability of well-conditioned athletes to release free fatty acids into the blood stream, indicates that training enhances fat metabolism.

In other words, you can train your body to metabolize fat for energy. In fact, there are many situations in which cyclists depend on fat metabolism. Riders in long road races, for example, where the pace in the peloton is conversational, are getting their energy primarily from fat metabolism.

How do you develop the ability to use fat efficiently as a fuel? It's easy. Every time you take a ride of four to five hours, you're training your body to switch from carbohydrates to fat as the primary source of energy.

Before you start eating a lot of fatty foods that will make you gain weight, realize that what we're talking about here is using the fat stored in muscle cells rather than general body fat, which is stored in a layer under the skin. The idea is to train your body to use the fat stores it already has. You do this with long-distance rides, not a high-fat diet.

Don't neglect protein needs

Since most of the energy for muscular work comes from carbohydrates and fats, why do you need protein?

It's true that little energy (1-10%) is derived from protein except in unusual circumstances, such as during long, endurance exercise or during a high-protein, low-carbohydrate diet. However, protein is necessary to make enzymes (the catalysts for all metabolic processes), as well as some hormones, antibodies, and plasma components that carry nutrients and help prevent too much water from leaving the blood.

Amino acids are the building blocks of protein. There are 22 amino acids (19 are found in foods) and they are divided into two groups, essential and nonessential. Essential amino acids are necessary for growth and development and must come from food. Nonessential amino acids can be produced by the body. Of the 10 essential amino acids, two are needed for growth during infancy and childhood, but are not essential during adulthood. So for an adult, there are eight essential amino acids. (Children and Juniors need more protein than adults to sustain growth and develop new tissue.)

Proteins are classified as either complete or incomplete. Complete proteins contain all the essential amino acids, while incomplete proteins are missing one or more. Complete proteins include milk, eggs, dairy products, meat, fish, and poultry. Incomplete proteins include grains, vegetables, and nuts.

In a diet containing both animal and plant protein, there is virtually no risk of missing essential amino acids. However, in a vegetarian diet the incomplete proteins must be combined in order to provide all the essential amino acids. It's important that this combining take place at each meal. Synthesis of complete protein will not occur unless all the necessary amino acids are present.

The conventional scientific view has long been that the protein requirements of athletes are not significantly different from non-exercising adults. However, current thinking questions the adequacy of the normal recommended dietary allowance (RDA) for protein when applied to endurance and strength-training athletes. The current U.S. RDA of .08 grams per kilogram of body weight per day may fall short of athletes' protein requirements.

Recent research indicates that protein breakdown provides more fuel for exercise than was previously believed. It's been calculated that the contribution of protein to exercise energy expenditure might range from 4% to 10%. While this amount may seem small, for athletes training for prolonged periods each day, the total protein requirement becomes significant.

Researchers now recommend that athletes consume 1.0-1.2 grams of protein per kilogram of body weight per day depending on age, sex, and energy expenditure. Some studies indicate that intake should go as high as 2.0 g/kg/day. This means that a cyclist weighing 160 pounds (72.5 kg) should consume 72-87 grams of protein per day, which shouldn't be difficult in a diet of 3,500-5,000 calories per day. (See table for protein content of various foods.)

PROTEIN CONTENT OF VARIOUS FOODS		
	Quantity	**Protein in grams**
Egg	1	7
Meat, fish, poultry	3 ounces	20-27
Milk	1 cup	8
Cheese	1 ounce	7-8
Peanut butter	2 tablespoons	7-8
Peanuts	2 tablespoons	6-7
Bread	1 slice	2-3
Fruit	1 cup	1
Vegetables	1 cup	4
Pasta	1 cup	4-6
Pizza	1 piece (medium)	8-10

The amount of protein you need depends on your age, weight, and energy expenditure but there are plenty of sources in the average diet.

What happens to excess protein? It is broken down into nitrogen and other by-products. The nitrogen is then excreted in the urine, while the other by-products are converted to carbohydrates and fat and used for immediate energy production or stored as fat.

Should your fuel be plant or animal?

The raging debate between vegetarians and meat-eaters can make interesting dinner conversation, but the truth is that no

DIETARY COMPARISON

Meat-and-potato meal	Kilocalories	Grams fat	Grams protein
10 oz. pot roast	818	113	56
1 med. baked potato	180	—	6
2 tbsp. margarine	200	24	—
2 pieces bread	140	2	4
1 lettuce salad	20	—	—
2 tbsp. French dressing	130	12	—
1 slice cherry pie	350	15	4
2 cups 2% milk	290	10	20
TOTAL	2128	176	90

Vegetarian meal	Kilocalories	Grams fat	Grams protein
1 med. baked potato	180	—	6
1 cup cooked carrots	45	—	1
½ cup cooked beans	30	—	2
1 lettuce salad	20	—	—
1 tsp. olive oil	125	14	—
1 tbsp. margarine	100	12	—
1 banana	100	—	1
1 apple	160	—	—
¼ cup cashews	195	16	6
TOTAL	1026	42	16

Neither of these meals is ideal for an active person. The vegetarian is not getting enough protein and probably not enough total calories. The non-vegetarian, on the other hand, has more than enough protein but may gain weight because of the greater total calories and runs a greater risk of atherosclerosis from the high amount of fat.

one can win the argument on nutritional grounds. Athletes can be successful using either diet. The key is to make intelligent food choices that provide all the necessary nutrients.

In order to better understand the nutritional advantages and problems of these two types of diet, let's look at the content of typical vegetarian and meat-and-potato meals (see table). We'll use for example a cyclist who weighs 165 pounds (75 kg) and requires 5,000 calories a day to maintain his weight.

The meat-and-potato meal contains 2,128 calories. If the cyclist ate like this three times a day, he would ingest an excess of 1,380 calories per day. At that rate, he would put on a pound of fat (3,500 calories) in three days, unless he rode more miles. The fact is, it's relatively easy to consume excess calories when large amounts of animal fats are eaten.

Another problem with this diet is that more than half the fat intake is in the form of saturated fat, which is a contributor to atherosclerosis. Fat is a necessary nutrient, but more should be consumed in the unsaturated form, which plays an important role in the metabolism of cholesterol.

The protein requirement for a whole day has been exceeded in the meat-and-potato meal alone. Though protein is a necessary nutrient, and meat contains all of the essential amino acids, this quantity is excessive. (It's also a waste of money, considering the high price of meat.)

Lettuce is the only food in that meal containing a significant amount of fiber. Fiber is necessary to stimulate contraction of the intestine, which causes food to be mixed. Mixing helps nutrients come into contact with the intestinal wall where they can be absorbed.

In addition to lacking fiber, a meat-and-potato diet may be missing some necessary nutrients, like those provided by a variety of fruits and vegetables. Though a meal like this one is often thought of as "well-balanced," we can now see that it isn't.

The lower half of the table depicts a naive vegetarian's meal. While the quantity of food appears to be large, it nevertheless has 650 calories less than the necessary amount. At the end of the day, a cyclist eating this way would be almost 2,000 calories short of his energy requirement. In a matter of just two days, he would lose a pound of body weight.

The problem of maintaining weight is common to many vegetarian cyclists. Because of the low caloric content of their food, they have to eat almost constantly during periods of hard training and racing. On the other hand, the extremely high fiber content in their diet increases the motility of the intestine, causing food to move through so fast that nutrients may not be fully used. This is why in hard stage races, where the energy requirements can be as high as 8,000 calories a day, vegetarians seem to be constantly eating or sitting in the restroom.

To obtain all essential amino acids, a vegetarian must take special care to eat a variety of whole grains, peas and beans, nuts, fruits, and vegetables. For example, grain products are low in lysine and peas are low in methionine (two essential amino acids), but when these foods are eaten together an adequate balance is provided.

Other nutrients, such as calcium, iron, and riboflavin (vitamin B_2) may be in short supply in a vegetarian diet. Also vitamin B_{12} is not found in plant foods. Lack of B_{12} causes pernicious anemia, which has an effect on the blood and nervous systems. To make sure they get these nutrients as well as ample complete protein, many vegetarian athletes are not strict vegans (eating no animal products whatsoever) but instead eat a lacto-ovo-vegetarian diet that includes dairy products and eggs.

The best diet for racing cyclists seems to lie between the extremes shown in the tables. The meat-and-potato rider should cut down on his intake of saturated fats and include more vegetable fats, fish, and poultry. The vegetarian should add one egg and two cups of 2% milk per day to his diet, along with 26 grams of protein, 16 grams of fat, and 370 calories.

The available evidence does not seem to favor one diet over the other in terms of athletic performance. The choice of a vegetarian or meat-and-potato diet is an individual one, but the mixing of both appears more nutritionally sound.

Are you too fat?

What if getting enough calories is not a problem for you? What if you have the opposite problem? For some cyclists, trying to lose weight and keep it off is hard and frustrating work. Let's face it — we can't all put in those 400- to 500-mile weeks like the pros and be able to eat just about anything we want without worrying about the caloric content.

Your weight is largely determined by genetics and depends on your body frame and your sex. Whether you can attain your ideal weight, or more correctly, body composition (amount of fat and amount of muscle), will depend on your lifestyle and eating habits.

Determining your ideal racing weight can be difficult. Charts and books on the subject are not good guides for athletes because athletes are usually lighter or more muscular than the average person. There's also a great variation within the sport itself. For example, road riders are usually lighter than the average individual, while track sprinters are usually heavier.

The body fat content of normally active men and women between the ages of 16 and 30 ranges from 14% in men to 22% in women. Some road cyclists, on the other hand, have less than 10% fat. Tests on elite professional road cyclists have shown some to be down around the 5-8% range. Although there are general guidelines for body fat percentage for cyclists, it's not always a good idea to compare yourself to other riders. They may feel comfortable and perform well weighing more or less than you do.

There are three common ways to measure body fat: skinfold measurement, underwater weighing, and elecrical impedance. Though there is a margin of error in all the tests, some are more accurate than others.

The most common way to measure body fat is with a skinfold caliper, which measures the amount of fat at different parts of the body. To assure accuracy, this test should only be performed by a qualified technician. The tester grabs a fold of skin (it should include two thicknesses of skin and subcutaneous fat but no muscle) between the thumb and forefinger. The tester then measures the depth of fat with a skinfold caliper, which determines the thickness of the fold in millimeters. This is done three times at each site and the average for each site is computed. The resulting measurements are then plugged into an equation to calculate body density and percent body fat. Be sure the equation used is derived from a population of athletes similar to you in age, sex, and sport activity, and of average height and weight.

Unfortunately, this test is only as accurate as the technician and his calipers. Metal calipers are best, but some of the better plastic ones are reasonably accurate. There is a 2-3% margin of error with even the best calipers.

Underwater weighing is considered to be the most accurate method of determining body composition. In hydrostatic weighing, you get into a tank of water in which a seat is connected to scales similar to those you find at the checkout counter of your local supermarket. You submerge yourself after blowing out all the air in your lungs and then try to hold steady while the technician gets an accurate reading on the scale.

This test is based on Archimedes' principle, which states that an object immersed in a fluid loses an amount of weight equivalent to the weight of fluid that is displaced. Since fat is lighter and more buoyant than bone or muscle, the greater your buoyancy, the lower your underwater weight will be. Fat weighs 0.9 grams per cubic centimeter, muscle weighs 1.05 grams, and lean tissue weighs 1.1 grams. Underwater weighing is not foolproof. If you don't blow out all the air in your lungs, you will be more buoyant and the test will show a higher percentage of body fat than you actually have.

Electrical impedance measurement of body composition is a space-age way to discover your body fat percentage. It works on the principle that fat doesn't contain much water but lean tissue does and that water conducts electricity.

During the test, electrodes are placed on your hands and feet. The electrodes are connected to a small portable computer and they send a small electrical current through your body for a few seconds. The computer calculates the amount of current lost and then works this into an equation — along with your height, weight, age, and sex — and estimates your lean body mass and body fat percentage. The more current that passes through the body, the more water-containing lean tissue there is. The computer then subtracts the lean body weight (which includes bones) from the total weight to figure out the fat weight and percentage of body weight.

How do you go about getting tested to determine your body fat percentage? Many universities, hospital labs, sportsmedicine clinics, and local YMCAs offer these tests.

Trim fat with diet and exercise

Once you've determined you need to lose fat, there are only three ways to accomplish that goal:

— Increase energy expenditure and keep food intake constant.

— Decrease food intake and keep energy expenditure constant.
— Combine the first and second methods.

The first method can be accomplished by excercise programs, the second by dieting.

How much energy do you expend while riding at different speeds? Let's assume that the average road racer weighs 170 pounds with bicycle. The graph depicts this cyclist's energy expenditure at different speeds. A cyclist weighing more than 170 pounds or one who is less efficient will move the curve

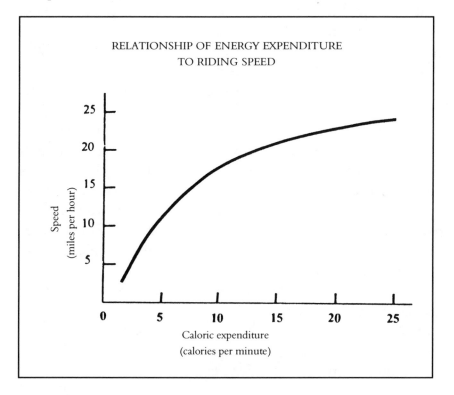

The curve shows the energy expended by a cyclist weighing 170 pounds with bicycle. Values for another rider will be greater or less depending on weight and fitness so the curve might move up or down.

upward. In other words, he will expend more energy. A rider weighing less than 170 pounds will move the curve down.

For example, in a four-and-a-half-hour road race in which the speed averages 23.5 mph, a 170-pound cyclist will use approximately 3,500-4,000 calories. Add to this the 1,500 calories per day required for normal activities and that cyclist will have to eat 5,000-5,500 calories that day to maintain body weight.

A pound of fat contains 3,500 calories. So if you were to not replace 2,000 of the calories that you burned each day in training, it would take about two days to lose one pound. This assumes you're eating enough to fuel your other daily activities. The problem is that it's hard to maintain a high level of training when the caloric deficit is this large.

A more workable solution is to create a deficit of 500-1,000 calories a day through decreased food intake and/or increased exercise. At this rate, you'll lose one to two pounds of fat per week.

If you're training hard, you should never consume less than 2,000 calories a day because with so few calories it's extremely difficult to get enough nutrients to sustain healthy bodily functions. Lower calorie intake will result in increasing use of muscle mass as an energy source. Consequently, you may feel sluggish, be more likely to overstress yourself, and be more susceptible to illness. Fasting should have no place in an athlete's diet.

Increasing your caloric output shouldn't be a concern if you're in training, for even if you're riding only an hour a day you're burning between 300 and 600 calories per hour depending upon the intensity of your effort.

If you're dieting, follow these guidelines:

— Cut down on foods that contain fats and and refined sugars.
— Select nutritious foods like vegetables, fruits, whole grains, beans and peas, lean meats, low-fat dairy products.
— Choose fresh, baked, boiled, broiled, or steamed foods without added fats or refined sugars.
— Regularly eat three to six small meals or snacks a day.
— Set realistic goals of losing one to two pounds of fat a week.
— Eat slowly. Never have food in your mouth at the same time you have food in your hand.
— Reject fad diets and quick-weight-loss gimmicks.
— Set a weight goal that lets you perform at your best.
— If you can't eat a balanced diet, supplement with a multiple vitamin-mineral tablet.

One prevalent misconception about exercise and weight control is that exercise increases the appetite. There is absolutely no evidence to support this claim.

Another false idea is that weight can be sweated off. This is only true for water weight, not fat. Exercising in extra clothes to induce heavy sweating will only cause temporary weight loss since it has nothing to do with body fat. Water does not contain calories, and fat weight can only be lost by burning calories.

9 / Vitamins and minerals

Vitamins contain no calories and provide no direct energy, yet without them life would be impossible. Like the spark plugs of an engine, vitamins ignite the cell metabolisms that harness, store, and use energy. Vitamins are divided into two groups: those soluble in fat and those soluble in water. Vitamins A, D, E, and K are in the first group, while C and the B-complex vitamins are in the second. This solubility determines whether the body can store a vitamin (fat soluble) or whether the vitamin needs to be supplied almost daily through food (water soluble).

Fat soluble vitamins are stored in the liver and fatty tissues of the body. If stores have been accumulated over a long period of time, you may be able to get along on inadequate amounts of these vitamins for several weeks, so supplementation is rarely needed. However, if you're not getting enough B and C vitamins, your athletic performance will decline in just a few weeks because those vitamins, though necessary for energy production, are not stored in the body. (If you ingest too much of these water soluble vitamins, the excess is excreted through the urine.)

Fat soluble vitamins

Vitamin A is essential for sound vision, resistance to infection, and maintenance of healthy skin and mucous membranes. Good sources are liver, dairy products, eggs, green leafy vegetables, and yellow vegetables such as carrots. The body usually stores enough vitamin A to cover any short-term deficiencies. Too much vitamin A may cause rough, dry skin and painful joint swelling.

Vitamin D is known as the sunshine vitamin because the body can produce it from a form of cholesterol in the skin during exposure to sunlight. Fortified dairy products and fish oils are also good sources. Vitamin D helps the body metabolize calcium and phosphorous to build bones and teeth.

Vitamin E is an antioxidant, which means it protects vitamins A and C and fatty acids from breaking down in the body. Vitamin E is required in such minute quantities that even the worst diet probably supplies adequate amounts. A normal, balanced diet provides 20-25 units, well above the body's needs. Sources include green leafy vegetables, vegetable oils, margarine, and rice. Too much vitamin E may lead to high blood pressure.

Vitamin K, produced in the intestine when certain bacteria are present, is essential for blood clotting and aids in fat digestion. It is also necessary for the production of glycogen in muscles. Large doses have not been shown to improve athletic performance in any way. Sources include green leafy vegetables, liver, alfalfa, wheat, rye, and fishmeal. Eating yogurt, kefir, and unsaturated fats helps to increase the amount produced.

Water soluble vitamins

B vitamins, found in meats (especially liver), brewer's yeast, nuts, and whole grains, are essential to the breakdown and utilization of carbohydrates and in fat metabolism — both very important for an athlete. They also regulate the growth of cells, including blood cells, and are necessary for the normal functioning of the nervous system.

Vitamin C, also known as ascorbic acid, is necessary to form collagen, a cementing substance that binds cells together. Vitamin C also aids the absorption of iron, the healing of wounds and fractures, and the production of energy sources during aerobic work. Important sources include most fresh vegetables and fruits (especially citrus) and their juices.

Do you need supplements?

There has been much discussion in the last few years about the need for athletes to take an antioxidant vitamin formula to protect their bodies from free radical damage and to help support the immune system while in hard training. In addition, there has been research conducted in the last few years showing the need for taking B and C supplements for the following reasons:

- Racing and training increase the rate of food metabolism, which also increases the use of vitamins and minerals.
- Eating large quantities of certain kinds of foods increases vitamin usage. For example, the need for thiamine (B_1) is increased when large amounts of carbohydrates are eaten.

— Racing cyclists often spend a lot of time traveling to events, which means they can't always eat a well-balanced diet. Also, the vitamin and mineral content of restaurant food is often lower than normal because of storage, processing, and cooking methods.
— Taking certain medications, such as aspirin, antibiotics, or anti-inflammatories, may decrease the body's absorption of vitamins.
— Taking oral contraceptives may deplete stores of B_6, B_{12}, folic acid, and C.
— Consuming high quantities of alcohol may impair absorption of B_1, folic acid, B_{12}, and C.

Almost every cyclist I know takes some vitamin supplements. Should you? If you're training hard, I recommend a general, over-the-counter vitamin supplement as insurance. Even if a vitamin just has a placebo effect for you, it's probably worthwhile. In other words, if you think that taking X, Y, and Z vitamins makes you a faster rider, I say go ahead and take them.

But don't overdo a good thing. If you take too much of any vitamin for a long enough time, your body gets used to that level. Then once you stop taking those large amounts, your body begins to show symptoms of deficiency even though you're still getting the recommended dietary allowance of those vitamins. So be careful about dosage.

Minerals play vital role

Your bones, teeth, and nails are mostly made of minerals, and minerals are essential to cell function. They control the flow of liquids in cell membranes and capillaries, and they regulate nerve tissue and muscle response. Minerals are also necessary to maintain proper acidity in the cells and they regulate blood volume and assist in water metabolism.

Minerals are excreted daily and must be replaced through food intake or supplements. Some minerals are needed in quantities larger than 100 mg a day while others, called trace minerals, are needed only in small amounts. The major minerals include calcium, phosphorus, magnesium, sodium, potassium, and chloride. Trace minerals include fluorine, chromium, manganese, cobalt, copper, iron, zinc, selenium, and iodine.

Are you calcium deficient?

Calcium is a critically important mineral, yet many people consume far too little of it. A recent U.S. government survey found that 25-50% of men ages 18-34 consume less than adequate amounts of calcium. Less than 33% of women ages 18-34 get adequate calcium, and after age 35, even fewer women (less than 25%) get all the calcium they need.

While 99% of the body's calcium is used in bones and teeth, small amounts are needed for muscle contraction, blood coagulation, hormone secretion, and nerve impulse transmission.

If your intake is inadequate, your body will maintain blood levels of calcium by dissolving and absorbing bone. You can only maintain calcium levels and strong bones if you produce adequate amounts of specific sex hormones and get enough vitamin D and calcium. When bone loss is excessive, the result can be osteoporosis — bones that are brittle, weak, and susceptible to fracture.

Exercise has been found to have a positive effect on the bones' ability to retain calcium and remain strong. Regular exercise can maintain bone density, while a sedentary lifestyle reduces the body's ability to use calcium and contributes to bone loss. Research has shown that people who are physically active throughout their lives have more bone mass than their more sedentary counterparts.

Women who have stopped menstruating (amenorrhea) may also suffer some bone weakening. Decreased menstruation is often associated with decreased production of estrogen, which is necessary for calcium absorption in females. Menopause also increases susceptibility to osteoporosis, because the body stops producing estrogen and the bones begin losing calcium at a faster rate.

Your best protection against osteoporosis or bone deterioration is to consume adequate levels of calcium. Daily intake should equal the amount found in four glasses of milk. The amount of calcium in one glass of milk is also found in half a cup of ice cream or cottage cheese, one cup of yogurt, or one ounce of hard cheese. Dark-green vegetables such as spinach and kale are also high in calcium, as are tofu and fish with soft bones such as tuna and sardines. And remember, adequate vitamin D intake is critical to the absorption of calcium. (Since most cyclists train outdoors, adequate vitamin D intake is usually not a problem.)

I recommend calcium supplements for cyclists who consume no dairy products and for those who take in less than two servings a day. Amenorrheic and post-menopausal female cyclists also probably need a supplement.

Calcium carbonate contains the highest percentage of calcium and is the cheapest calcium supplement available. Calcium carbonate is found in antacids such as Tums and Antacid, and in supplements such as Caltrate 600, Biocal, and Cal Sup. But read the labels carefully for calcium content. For example, since Caltrate 600 contains only 40% calcium, you'll have to take four tablets to meet the RDA.

Don't use calcium supplements made of bone meal or dolomite, because they may contain lead and other heavy metals. Lead accumulates in the bones of the animals that are used for these supplements, and the supplements may contain as much as 15-20 parts per million for lead — a dangerous amount.

Phosphorus compounds are the principal catalysts in muscle contraction, and are essential in the conversion of glycogen to glucose. However, a deficiency of phosphorus is unlikely since the mineral is found in most plant and animal foods. Excellent sources include beans, cheese, eggs, lentils, liver, milk, peanuts, and whole wheat.

Sodium salts are necessary to preserve the balance between calcium and potassium that maintains normal heart action. They play an important role in the electrical balance between the inside and the outside of a cell, and they guard against excessive water loss from tissues. You lose some sodium in sweating, but even under extreme conditions you can replace such losses by salting your food more heavily or by consuming an electrolyte drink. In cases of muscle cramping caused by salt depletion, you should replace salt only in conjunction with adequate fluids. No minimum daily requirement has been set for sodium. However, athletes are rarely deficient in this mineral since it is found in nearly all foods, especially kelp, celery, romaine lettuce, and watermelon.

Chloride, found in body fluids in conjunction with sodium, has two major functions: it helps maintain proper blood acidity, and it helps the formation of hydrochloric acid for food digestion. Most chloride is taken into the body in the form of sodium chloride, more commonly known as table salt.

Potassium is the principal mineral within body cells. Along with sodium, it determines the amount of water held in tissues. Potassium is essential for the proper functioning of muscle and nerve cells. A deficiency may cause muscular weakness and fatigue. Fresh and dried fruit, beans, sunflower seeds, and nuts are excellent sources.

Iron is essential for top performance

Although technically a trace mineral, iron is a critically important substance, and cyclists who are iron deficient or anemic are doomed to second-class performances. Just ask 1989 Tour de France winner Greg LeMond. Three weeks before the Tour he found himself riding inexplicably poorly. A physical exam revealed he had anemia and a low iron count. Iron supplements were immediately prescribed and LeMond's performance improved within days. He called it a turning point in his season.

Iron is vital for the production of hemoglobin, the oxygen-carrying component of the blood. A deficiency of hemoglobin hampers the transportation of oxygen from the lungs to the muscles. Reduced oxygen to the muscles means inadequate burning of carbohydrates and fats, and the end result is poor performance.

If your blood test for hemoglobin falls below a certain range, you're considered anemic. Traditionally the standard has been 14 grams per 100 milliliters for men and 12 grams per 100 milliliters for women. However, such standards may be too low for athletes, who need to perform at a maximum level. Many scientists now believe that any hemoglobin concentration below 15-16 grams is too low for a competitive athlete.

Even if you're not technically anemic, you may have an iron deficiency that is limiting your performance. The average cyclist, male or female, normally loses 0.9 milligrams of iron in daily activity. Women lose an additional 15-45 mg each time they menstruate. Hard-training cyclists may double their loss of iron through excessive sweating.

Many of us simply do not eat enough iron-rich foods to compensate for these losses. Our bodies absorb only a small fraction of the iron in our food anyway, which means we have to eat a lot to get an adequate iron supply.

The RDA for iron is 15 mg a day for women and 10 mg for men. The average diet, however, contains only about 6 mg of iron per 1,000 calories. So you must be very conscious of the foods you eat to ensure that they are rich in iron. Good sources include red meats (especially liver), whole grain foods, nuts, and dried fruits. Vegetarian cyclists are especially susceptible to iron deficiency and should make an extra effort to eat plenty of iron-rich foods.

Normally the body maintains a relatively large reserve of iron in bone marrow. If there is a temporary reduction in intake or absorption of iron, or if there is a loss of blood, the reserve in the marrow can be called on to cover the imbalance. A continued shortage of iron, however, may lead to depletion of the marrow stores.

The most common method of measuring iron reserves is with a serum ferritin test. The measurement is in nanograms (ng) of iron, or billionths of a gram, per milliliter of blood. Again the question is: what is adequate for the cyclist? According to Douglas Clement, who has reseached the subject extensively with athletes, a test result below 12 ng/ml indicates you're unquestionably deficient. Below 20 is probably a latent deficiency, and below 30 may be pre-latent. A measurement between 30 and 60 is suspicious. Anything over 60 is fine.

Again, what is adequate for one cyclist may be insufficient for another. World-class athletes have been found to have values from as low as 11 ng/ml to as high as 300 ng/ml.

You can supplement your iron, but carefully

Serum ferritin tests should be taken every 6-12 months to keep track of your blood profile. You might also want to consult a nutritionist to determine your iron intake. If a deficiency is suspected, you might need nutritional counseling or iron supplementation.

But remember: the best way to increase iron is through iron-rich food. If a doctor recommends a supplement, you can take ferrous gluconate three to four times a week, 30 minutes after eating. But be careful. Iron supplements should be taken only under medical supervision because they can be dangerous. The ingestion of massive amounts of iron can cause sudden death. The second-most-common cause (after aspirin) of accidental poisoning of small children is ingestion of iron supplements or vitamins with iron. An adult version of overload is called hemochromatosis. In this case iron overload is characterized by deposits of iron-containing pigment in many tissues, resulting in tissue damage.

10 / Water and athletic performance

Many riders will go into a 50- to 75-mile race with only 2 water bottles, yet on a hot day they may lose as much as 8 to 10 pounds of water through sweating. Even if they drink both bottles (about 40 ounces), only about 2.5 pounds of lost fluid is replaced. The resulting fluid deficiency will put a severe strain on the circulatory system, which is about 70% water.

Water, the original fluid replacement

Water is essential for sound health and top athletic performance. It's the primary component in most cells and performs many vital functions, including transporting nutrients to cells and removing waste by-products.

Water also acts as a temperature regulator, taking heat from the cells and transporting it to the skin, where it's dispersed into the air. During heavy exercise, heat is primarily dissipated through sweating, and it's not unusual to sweat away more than five pounds of water during a two-hour bike race. Since a loss of fluid equaling just 2% of your body weight can seriously impair muscle function, you must avoid dehydration and its potentially harmful effects.

When water is lost, blood plasma has a limited capacity to carry nutrients (glucose, fats, oxygen, etc.) to the working muscles and to remove the by-products of metabolism (carbon dioxide, heat, lactic acid, etc.). When sweat loss greatly exceeds fluid replacement, blood flow to the extremities decreases. If heavy sweating continues, blood volume drops. As a result the heart is able to pump less blood per stroke, so the beat rate must increase to get blood where it's needed. Body temperatures continue to climb to dangerous levels, which can lead to heat exhaustion or heat stroke.

Know the signs of heat illness

Heat exhaustion is characterized by a lack of circulation to the extremities. The cyclist becomes weak and dizzy and his skin feels cold and clammy to the touch. He may sweat profusely. Body temperature is usually normal but blood pressure may be low. These symptoms may be accompanied by headache, restlessness, and vomiting.

If these characteristics are present, get the rider to a cool area and keep him quiet. Loosen his clothing and place him in a head-low position. Keep his body warm to prevent the onset of shock. Make him drink fluids (fruit juice is ideal). If he doesn't improve fairly rapidly, or if he gets worse, get medical help. An intravenous isotonic saline solution may be necessary; it definitely will be if the rider becomes unconscious.

An even more dangerous form of heat illness, heat stroke (also called sun stroke), can be fatal. Heat stroke is caused by the failure of the body's heat-regulating mechanisms. Signs of heat stroke include cessation of sweating, headache, numbness, tingling, confusion, and sudden delirium or coma. There may also be muscle convulsions. Pupils are dilated and breathing and pulse rate are rapid. Blood pressure is often elevated, and body temperature usually exceeds 105 degrees.

If these symptoms are present, the cyclist must be stripped of clothing and cooled down immediately. The best way is in a bathtub filled with ice water. Remove him from the water when his temperature falls to 103 degrees. If you can't get him to a tub, lay him down with his head elevated and apply cold water and wet cloths to his body. Fan him vigorously and massage his skin. Have him drink cold fluids. Get him to a hospital as soon as possible, keeping his body wet on the way with cold water or rubbing alcohol. At the hospital he may receive infusions of normal saline solution. For the next several days he should be watched for signs of fluid imbalance and kidney failure.

Although it may be impossible to offset all water lost in sweating, even partial replacement can minimize the problems of overheating and reduce the threat of circulatory collapse. Here are three rules to follow while training or racing in hot weather:

— Drink 13-20 ounces 15 minutes before riding.
— Drink 4-5 ounces every 10-15 minutes during the ride.
— Weigh yourself every morning and keep a chart. Rapid changes in weight are most likely due to fluid loss. Don't allow yourself to get into a state of chronic dehydration.

Thirst is not always a good indicator of your need to drink. In hot weather, make sure to have plenty of fluids between meals and in the evening.

Carbohydrate drinks may boost your energy

The fluid of choice for athletes used to be plain water because it empties quickly from the stomach (fluid is absorbed primarily through the large intestine). However, recent studies have shown that the addition of substances known as carbohydrate polymers don't significantly decrease the rate of gastric emptying of fluids. These polymers are now used in commercial sports drinks like Cytomax, Hydrafuel, Gatorade, and others, which can fill your fluid and energy replacement needs at the same time. (A solution of 6-10% carbohydrates works best.)

Water is the primary substance lost in sweating, but it's not the only one. Small amounts of mineral salts known as electrolytes are also secreted, and recent research suggests that such losses may be associated with muscle cramping and fatigue.

If you lose nine pounds of sweat during a long race or training ride (about a 5.5% loss in a 165-pound rider), you lose roughly 6-8% of your body's stores of sodium and chloride (the primary two electrolytes involved with maintaining the water content outside the cells). At the same time potassium and magnesium would decrease by less than 1%. These percentages seem small, but research indicates they may be enough to cause muscle cramps and intolerance to heat.

When you sweat heavily, you lose more water than electrolytes, causing the concentration of electrolytes in the body to become higher. If you undergo several days of hot-weather exercise, your body will actually begin conserving electrolytes by secreting smaller amounts through the urine. Therefore, in heavy exercise the need to replace water and carbohydrates is greater than the immediate demand for electrolytes.

The evidence seems to say that a cyclist who eats a well-balanced diet will adequately replenish the electrolytes lost in daily sweating. However, many commercial sports drinks also tout their electrolyte content. Should you avoid them? No. As long as their mineral content is not too high (which slows gastric emptying), you should look on them as good fluid replacement with a little extra insurance.

Beware the bonk

Dehydration, overheating, and loss of electrolytes are all among the causes that contribute to the cycling malady known as the bonk. You may be all-too familiar with the symptoms: sudden and extreme weakness and fatigue (even your easiest gear seems too hard to pedal), emptiness in the stomach, maybe even cramping. Once the bonk strikes, it's impossible to maintain your pace.

One of the other causes behind the bonk may be low blood glucose levels. Blood glucose is the only energy source used by the brain and nervous system, neither of which can store any appreciable amounts. Instead, they must depend on a constant supply from the blood stream.

Blood glucose levels are primarily regulated by the liver, which contains large reserves. However, research indicates that extended exercise may deplete the liver's glucose stores. In several studies, subjects exercised to exhaustion on a bicycle ergometer. This resulted in reduced levels of blood glucose. After ingestion of 200 grams of glucose and 15 minutes of rest, the subjects were able to ride for an additional time. This suggests that exhaustion may sometimes be a central nervous system phenomenon and not the result of depleted muscle fuel stores.

As a long ride or race progresses cyclists frequently eat solid food in an attempt to avoid the bonk, but in order to digest food the stomach must work harder and receive a greater blood supply. This causes a diversion of blood away from leg muscles where it is needed most.

A more efficient method may be to use carbohydrate loading before the event (see chapter 8), then drink sugared fluids or high-calorie carbohydrate drinks during the race. Any of the commercial products mentioned earlier would work well.

Many cyclists believe that excess lactic acid build-up in muscle cells also contributes to the bonk, but studies don't support this theory. Because lactic acid can be removed from working muscles, it is not the cause of exhaustion experienced in a long road race.

Alcohol won't help your cycling

I'm frequently asked whether cyclists should drink alcohol. As with most foods or beverages, moderation is the key.

Alcohol contains about 7 calories per gram as compared to 4 calories per gram of carbohydrate and 9 calories per gram of fat. In general, the calories found in beer, wine, or liquor are empty calories, meaning they have little nutritional value. A 12-ounce can of regular beer has about 150 calories and 13-14 grams of carbohydrates, 13 grams of fat, and 1 gram of protein. It also contains some calcium, potassium, and B vitamins. Light beer has roughly one-half to two-thirds these amounts.

As far as the body is concerned, alcohol is a foreign substance, unlike fats and carbohydrates, and cannot be stored or used in its original form for energy. It must first be metabolized in the liver and converted into acetaldehyde and then to acetate before it can be used by the liver or muscles. However, the muscles have a much harder time using acetate than glucose for fuel, so it's a mistake to think that alcohol can provide a rapid source of energy during cycling.

Alcohol has other negative effects during exercise. Processing alcohol impairs the liver's ability to produce new glucose from lactate. Research has shown that even moderate doses of alcohol reduce the amount of glucose released by the liver and limit the amount of blood glucose used by the muscles. Since the need for glucose increases during exercise, alcohol consumption can result in earlier fatigue.

Also, alcohol is a depressant. Though some athletes say it helps calm their nerves and reduce pain sensation, it also adversely affects perceptual-motor activity. Your reaction time, balance, vision, and coordination deteriorate even with low levels of consumption. We all know the dangers of driving a car with a too-high blood alcohol content; the same holds true while riding a bike.

In addition, excessive alcohol acts as a diuretic. Instead of replacing fluids, you will urinate more frequently and actually dehydrate yourself. So during exercise, stick to water or energy drinks, or drink one of the non-alcohol varieties of beer on the market.

Drinking beer won't do much for your cycling, but doctors have found that it may contribute to your overall health. Some research indicates that moderate amounts of alcohol — the equivalent of two beers or a cocktail a day — increases the level of high-density lipoproteins in the blood. These lipoproteins help protect the body from cardiovascular disease by serving two important functions. They coat the inside of the arteries and prevent fatty deposits from building up, and they actually help dissolve fatty deposits when they do occur.

The problem with emphasizing the "alcohol solution" to the blood balance problem is that the cure may be worse than the disease. Too much alcohol can lead to other problems and should not take the place of a sound exercise program and a low-fat, low-cholesterol diet.

HEALTH

11 / Keeping healthy

No matter how careful you are, at some point in your cycling career, you're likely to suffer a cycling injury. If home remedies don't work, your best bet is to seek medical help from a physician who is familiar with sportsmedicine. You may not find one knowledgeable about cycling *per se*, but a sports doctor will understand the physical, psychological, and emotional differences between athletes and sedentary individuals.

The problem with many general physicians is that they aren't familiar with the lab results an athlete will produce. For example, a trained cyclist's blood test may show below-average red cell values. The doctor may diagnose anemia. It is now known, however, that athletes develop an increased blood volume from training, which may result in proportionally lower red cell count. The cyclist may actually have a higher number of total red blood cells than a more sedentary individual because the increased plasma dilutes the percentages.

General physicians are often not aware that injuries to athletes may require nonstandard treatments. What's more, some treatments that normally produce good results may actually have an adverse affect on athletes. For example, doctors commonly prescribe cortisone to relieve tendinitis. But cortisone reduces the blood supply to the tendon, increasing the likelihood that it will tear under strenuous exercise.

I recommend searching for a physician who is also an athlete. He or she may even have had problems similar to yours. Call your local high school or college trainer and ask for names of doctors experienced in treating athletic injuries, or contact the nearest medical school, which will have contacts with doctors who work with athletes. If all else fails, call the local chapter of the American College of Sports Medicine, or contact their main office at Post Office Box 1440, Indianapolis, Indiana 46306-1440.

If your injury involves bone or muscle, contact a sports orthopedist. To find those closest to you, write the American Orthopaedic Society of Sports Medicine, 430 North Michigan Avenue, Chicago, Illinois 60611.

Get a preseason physical

Every athlete should have a preseason physical examination. Even if you feel perfectly healthy, you should see a doctor to find out if you're physically fit for serious training. Any irregularities in cardiovascular, neurological, orthopedic, or respiratory functions can be discovered during the exam and treated before the season begins.

Your physical should take place at least one month before the start of the season to allow time for any needed treatments. Make sure your doctor gets your complete medical and injury history — including prior and current medical problems and previous injuries — as well as symptoms related to exercise, such as wheezing or lightheadedness. If you fill out a history form yourself, be sure you understand all the terms used.

The exam should include blood tests to determine red blood cell, hemoglobin, hematocrit, and white blood cell counts, which establish your general state of health. These are especially useful if you're having chronic problems with training or have symptoms of staleness. The exam also provides a baseline for later reference in case of illness or injury. If any abnormalities are found, your physician can suggest changes in diet, sleep, rest, and training regimens.

A complete preseason physical should discover:

— Any medical or orthopedic problems that would be aggravated by cycling or by early season activities like weight training.
— Any medical or orthopedic problems that require further evaluation and/or therapy before you begin hard exercise.
— Any structural characteristics that predispose you to injury and that may require preventive devices such as orthotics. (Young athletes should pay particular attention to this.)
— Your level of physical fitness and if any specific conditioning programs are needed.

Don't ignore eye problems

When you make the appointment for your preseason physical, be sure to schedule a trip to your eye doctor as well. Athletes all too often neglect proper eye care. I know many cyclists who are constantly working to improve their equipment or who absolutely have to keep up with the latest training techniques. Unfortunately, they ignore a vital key to cycling success — their eyes.

A five-year vision study involving more than 3,000 high school and college athletes found that many had such poor vision as to be considered legally blind when they competed without their glasses. In fact, 230 of the athletes who wore prescription lenses (eyeglasses or contact lenses) failed to pass the visual examination at all, even with their glasses.

Athletes with vision problems risk serious and permanent damage to themselves and others. How often have such riders been unable to see an obstacle and react fast enough to avoid an accident? A sprinter with poor peripheral vision may be at a disadvantage in a closing stretch. Visual fatigue can tire your body during a long race and leave you accident-prone.

If you have to squint to see clearly in the distance, you could have a vision problem. If you're constantly rubbing your eyes or getting headaches, excessive eye redness, or tearing after a ride, you may be suffering from visual fatigue.

See your optometrist or opthalmologist and find out. If he or she discovers that you need corrective lenses, you have several options.

Contact lenses or glasses?

Contact lenses have been an important advance in opthalmology. Their greatest benefit to the athlete is that they become, in effect, a part of the eye itself and so move with it. Another advantage is that they don't restrict peripheral vision, whereas eyeglasses can reduce peripheral vision by as much as 15-25%, depending on the frame style. Contact lenses also enhance depth perception. And, unlike regular glasses, contacts don't normally cloud up during temperature changes. They can also be tinted to reduce glare.

One of the main drawbacks to contact lenses is that they're more expensive than regular glasses. Other serious disadvantages are eye irritation caused by dust getting under the lens (a definite problem in a long road race) and the possibility of the lens becoming dislodged by wind.

About 15 years ago, a new product came into widespread use: soft contact lenses. They were thought to be the solution to many of the problems associated with hard lenses. They seldom slip, pop off, or cause abrasions of the eye. They are larger, more comfortable, and less sensitive to light, wind, and dust.

But soft lenses also have problems. They require extra care and are expensive. They can cloud up if not cleaned in the proper solution, and they must be handled carefully because they can be easily torn. And you need special equipment to care for them.

Contact lenses are one option, but many athletes prefer to stick with tried-and-true glasses. If you wear glasses, choose a design made with the athlete in mind. Plastic lenses are highly recommended because they're harder to break. They are also as much as 50% lighter than the same prescription in glass. Plastic lenses also give less surface glare and are less apt to fog up. (Fogging can be prevented by cleaning the glasses with a steam-preventing, anti-static lens cleaner.) Photochromatic lenses, which take on a brownish cast when exposed to ultraviolet rays, are helpful in reducing sun glare.

If you wear glasses or contacts, carry a spare pair with you to races in case you lose or damage the ones you're wearing. Another good precaution is to get a copy of your prescription to take with you on extended trips. This is especially important if you're traveling overseas.

Asthma and the cyclist

Cycling challenges all of us to reach new heights of health and fitness, but special health problems like asthma or insulin-dependent diabetes make that challenge even greater.

1996 Olympic team member and previous World Champion in the Individual Pursuit, Mike McCarthy, had more than the usual hurdles to overcome in his pursuit to make the Olympic Team. McCarthy has asthma. Yet, with proper training and medical care, he was able to overcome any limitations this asthma might have presented.

People who don't normally suffer from asthma — individuals who under most circumstances are non-allergic — can still get asthmatic symptoms brought on by exercise or breathing cold air. This condition is known as exercise-induced asthma.

The symptoms of exercise-induced asthma usually occur several minutes after starting continuous exercise or within five minutes of finishing. Breathlessness may be severe both during and after the exercise and may be accompanied by chest pain or tightness. Breathing is often labored and wheezing is audible.

Exercise-induced asthma is caused by a cooling of the air passages as air flows in and out of the lungs. Breathing dry air is the most likely cause of the cooling. When you exercise in a place where the relative humidity is low, increased amounts of moisture evaporate from the air tubes. It's no wonder exercise-induced asthma occurs more often in winter — not only is the outdoor air colder, but the indoor air is usually drier.

Here are a few guidelines to follow if you're asthmatic:

— Take medication or inhalants before cycling to prevent an attack and carry them with you on your rides.
— If a specific allergy induces attacks, avoid the cause.
— Keep drinking lots of fluids.
— Avoid cold, dry, outdoor air. Many asthmatic athletes have found that wearing a surgical mask or face covering prevents cold air from reaching the lungs and triggering a reaction. Carry a bandanna if you expect the temperature to drop during your ride. In winter

consider riding indoors on a home trainer with a room humidifier running.

— Take plenty of time to warm up on your rides. Don't charge immediately up a steep hill. Ride easy at first and let your heart and lungs adjust to the demands of exercise.

Asthmatics must recognize their own tolerances for exercise, pace themselves properly, and rest when necessary.

Know what's in your medication

Competitive cyclists need to know what's in asthma medications, because the drugs may cause a positive drug test. The International Olympic Committee prohibits the use of ephedrine, isopreterenol, isoetharine, epinephrine, decongestants, and related compounds. The inhaled beta sympathomimetics (Albuterol, Terbutaline), cromolyn, theophylline, and corticosteroids are on the approved list. (Cromolyn sodium drugs are used to prevent attacks and must therefore be taken before exercise.)

Balancing cycling and diabetes

Cyclists with diabetes must create a balance between insulin, physical activity, and food intake in order to keep blood sugar levels in the proper range.

Diabetes is characterized by a deficiency of insulin, a hormone essential for the metabolism of glucose, which is the chief energy source for muscles. Insulin facilitates the absorption of glucose into tissues by changing the permeability of cell membranes.

There are two major classifications of diabetes. Type I (juvenile-onset) diabetes usually appears before the age of 20, but can also develop later in life. It is more common in men than women and is believed to be caused by a genetic defect in the ability of the pancreas to produce insulin. Being physically fit and active does not prevent it.

Type II (non-insulin dependent) diabetes usually strikes people who are overweight and past age 40. However, it too can appear at any age. This type of diabetes is thought to result when tissue targets (that is, muscles) become less sensitive to insulin. This causes excess production and release of insulin by the pancreas, which eventually exhausts itself from overwork.

Type II diabetes can be controlled through diet or treated orally with drugs that control secretion of pancreatic insulin.

Type I diabetics must inject insulin into their blood to compensate for the body's deficiency. If they don't, glucose remains in the blood, in effect starving the body's cells, causing lethargy and grogginess. Fortunately, diabetics can regulate blood sugar levels by taking synthetic insulin injections in balance with diet and activity. (The dose required to control the diabetes depends on the severity and type of insulin deficiency, as well as age and body size.)

What happens when a diabetic takes up cycling? Although riding a bike can't cure diabetes or make insulin injections unnecessary, it does help lower blood sugar and can lessen the amount of insulin needed. Exercise somehow makes it easier for insulin to move glucose out of the blood into the cells, so less insulin is needed.

The lower need for insulin can also be cumulative. That is, after several months of training, a given insulin level yields a larger decline in blood glucose than it does in an untrained individual.

Twenty years ago, few physicians would have allowed their diabetic patients to engage in anything as strenuous and exhausting as competitive cycling, but such restrictions are no longer necessary. Today, with the aid of monitoring kits, blood glucose levels can be determined in a few minutes. This allows diabetics the freedom to experiment with different training methods and to alter their insulin injections and diet accordingly. But remember, don't change any injection schedule or diet pattern before obtaining advice from your physician.

If you're diabetic, be sure to eat before and during exercise. During long rides, drink a dilute glucose-and-water solution every 15 to 20 minutes. The water helps prevent heat exhaustion and promotes fast emptying of the stomach. The sugar will prevent hypoglycemia (low blood sugar). Also, use your stomach or arms as injection sites rather than your legs, because if the injection is administered in a muscle group that is being actively exercised, the absorption rate of insulin is accelerated and may cause hypoglycemia.

If you're a diabetic, alternate light and heavy training days, eating extra carbohydrates as necessary to meet your calorie demands. You should avoid carbohydrate loading because of problems with glucose metabolism.

Physical activity's effect on insulin and blood sugar regulation doesn't end when you stop riding. After a heavy workout, you may need an extra snack before bed to avoid hypoglycemia. You may also find that you need to alter the schedule of your insulin injections. (Most diabetic athletes feel more comfortable dividing their daily injections into two or more sessions.)

Recognize the warning signs

Learn to recognize the signs of hypoglycemia while training or competing. It usually occurs when there's an overabundance of insulin, often in combination with inadequate food intake. You'll experience hunger, faintness, nausea, double vision, and muscular weakness. Eating sugar usually leads to rapid recovery. Make sure you carry candy bars or some form of sugar tablets with you on all your rides.

Hyperglycemia, or abnormally high levels of blood sugar, can also occur during training, usually when food levels are adequate but insulin levels are low. (Such a condition is usually preceded by an illness that alters insulin demand.) If you experience hyperglycemia, your skin will be dry and flushed. Your mouth will be dry and you will be severely thirsty, along with needing to urinate frequently. You will look ill, and your breathing will be forced and irregular. In such cases, insulin must be administered immediately along with water.

Diabetic cyclists should carry diabetic identification cards at all times, and shouldn't train alone. Inform your fellow cyclists of your condition and tell them what to do in case of an emergency. Always carry a readily available source of carbohydrates.

Some facts about cholesterol

Many riders believe that, thanks to cycling, their chances of heart disease are virtually nil. They've heard or read reports that imply that the more physically active you are, the less likely you are to suffer from heart ailments.

In fact, several factors have been cited as possible contributing causes of heart attacks: excess weight, high blood pressure, smoking, and high levels of blood cholesterol. Cyclists score well on the first three, being typically lean, non-smoking, and having normal blood pressure. But the findings on exercise's effects on cholesterol levels are less clear.

To understand how cholesterol, fats, and lipoproteins relate to exercise and heart disease, we need to review a little biochemistry and physiology.

Cholesterol is an essential part of cell walls, sex hormones, and bile salts. Early research found it to be a main constituent of plaques (soft fatty accumulation on the inner wall of arteries.) The conclusion was that dietary cholesterol was the villain in heart disease.

Triglycerides are a form of fat that is stored in the body primarily as an energy source. Both cholesterol and triglycerides are moved through the body via the bloodstream. They do not dissolve in the blood, but are carried with the help of proteins known as the lipoproteins.

Recent findings indicate that the amount of cholesterol carried in the blood by lipoproteins may have more impact on heart disease than total cholesterol. In fact, cholesterol is transported by three different forms of lipoproteins. They can't be seen by the naked eye, but scientists have classified them by their density:

— Very low-density lipoproteins (VLDL), the largest and least dense.
— Low-density lipoproteins (LDL), middle sized.
— High-density lipoproteins (HDL), the smallest.

VLDL are composed primarily of triglycerides and very little cholesterol, so a high blood-triglyceride level means a high VLDL level. The other two, LDL and HDL, carry most of the cholesterol, so a high level of blood cholesterol can mean large amounts of LDL or HDL, or both.

What effect do these various lipoproteins have on your health? Little is known about the consequences of high VLDL levels, but having a low VLDL level (with lower blood levels of triglycerides) seems to be preferred. A high LDL level has been linked with atherosclerosis (hardening of the arteries) and heart attacks.

But it's the facts about HDL concentrations that are the most eye-opening. Consider the following recent findings:

— Heart-attack victims have a lower than normal HDL level.
— Human babies and laboratory animals that have elevated HDL levels are resistant to heart disease.
— Women, who have high HDL concentrations, have fewer heart attacks than men.
— Endurance athletes (marathon runners, cross-country skiers, cyclists) have relatively high HDL levels.

The hypothesis is that all three lipoproteins travel through the blood vessels at high speed, being jostled against the walls by various materials in the blood. Some of the LDL infiltrate the vessel walls and deposit their cholesterol. As a result, atherosclerosis may develop. HDL, on the other hand, is thought to absorb cholesterol constantly from the walls and return it to the liver to help produce bile (a substance that aids in absorption and digestion of fats).

When you hear the term "blood cholesterol level," remember that this is the total cholesterol carried by all three lipoproteins. For example, two cyclists with identical cholesterol levels of 250 milligrams per deciliter of blood may have totally different lipoprotein profiles.

Physicians have recently begun to look at the ratio of total blood cholesterol to HDL cholesterol — the lower the ratio, the less risk of coronary disease. Studies on runners and cyclists indicate that exercise may cause a beneficial increase in the HDL level.

How about people who are in their 30s or 40s before they begin a training program? Will their HDL value improve? Several studies indicate that it will. However, the definitive answer may not be available until some long-term studies are completed.

The current theory is that regular exercise appears to produce beneficial changes in lipoproteins. This is in addition to the role exercise plays in controlling body weight and blood pressure. So it can be said with some certainty that cycling may act as preventive medicine in the fight against heart disease.

Endorphins, the natural high

In the early '70s, scientists discovered that when a certain part of the brain was stimulated, test subjects had a sense of pain relief. Several years later, they found a compound in the brain tissue that had pain-relieving properties. Similar to morphine but even more effective against pain, it was given the name endorphin.

Evidence suggests that stress and exercise cause the release of endorphin. After any intense aerobic exercise, the body attempts to relieve pain by releasing endorphin into the system. Endorphin has been directly linked to the "runner's high" — a sense of well-being during strenuous exercise — and may cause addiction to exercise. Endorphin may also be the reason why endurance athletes say muscle tension is released after training. In fact, daily exercise may even lower the stress level of life in general.

The connection between exercise and endorphin is interesting, not only for what it may say about the calming effect of cycling, but because endorphin has also been linked to such varied body functions as heat regulation, breakdown of body fat, and appetite. Changes in these functions have also been associated with endurance training. Recent studies on the body's response to training have reinforced the link between endorphin and exercise.

In a study at the University of New Mexico, researchers found a large increase in endorphin levels in 15 male runners after a 46-km mountain race. These levels, which varied among the individuals, remained elevated for two hours after the event. In another study, the blood plasma of long-distance runners was tested for endorphin before and after easy and hard running. The researchers discovered that the release of endorphin appeared to be related to the intensity of exercise. They also found that endorphin returned to the baseline level in as little as 30 minutes. These findings, along with those from New Mexico, indicate that the type of exercise determines both the amount of endorphin put into the system, and the length of time before it is used up.

Because endorphin decreases sensitivity to pain, some people think that it may cause athletes to ignore a minor injury until it becomes major. As yet, there is no substantial evidence to confirm this theory. The release of endorphin might explain the mood improvement following exercise, and the depression experienced by a regular exerciser who misses several workouts.

Researchers tell us that we all ride with an elevated endorphin level. This may be the very reason many of us continue to ride.

12 / Treating illness

Has this ever happened to you? After months of training, just when you're rounding into top form, you get struck down by one of the most ubiquitous diseases known to man — the common cold.

It may be no coincidence that peak fitness and illness so often go hand in hand. In fact, when training loads are particularly heavy and reserves lag, athletes may be even more susceptible to colds than the general population. At the 1994 Winter Olympic Games more than 90% of the visits to physicians were for the treatment of the common cold.

Taking care of the common cold

Colds are caused by viruses that invade the lining of the nose and throat. (Incapable of living on their own, viruses need the human body in order to survive.) At its worst, a cold may cause muscle aches, pains, fever, and headaches.

Exposure to a cold can occur simply through hand contact with a contaminated surface or an infected person. That's why people who work or live in crowded conditions are especially susceptible to colds.

Are you more likely to catch a cold when you feel chilled, such as after a hard ride or race? No. There is absolutely no evidence that cold weather, dampness, or changes in temperature will lead to colds. The only reason for not cycling on a cold, damp day is that it is unpleasant, not that you're more likely to catch a cold.

The onset of a cold is usually marked by dryness or burning of the nose. Later a watery nasal discharge appears. At this point we usually begin our treatment with nasal sprays, antihistamines, and decongestants. Despite the relief they offer from symptoms, these drugs do nothing to the virus, nor do they prevent future complications. In fact, most of the time they just make you feel tired and lethargic.

Vitamin C has been touted as a cold cure-all but, in fact, it hasn't been shown to be any more effective in treating cold symptoms than any other product, nor does it make you less susceptible to colds.

The most effective treatment for a cold is to liquify and warm the mucus in your lungs so that it will flow more freely and carry more of the virus tissue debris to your mouth. Adequate humidity in your living and working area is important. Use a home humidifier to help keep the relative humidity from dropping below 35%. An alternative would be to sit for 20 minutes or so in your bathrooom with the hot shower running, or lie in a warm bath and breathe warm, wet air. Drinking warm fluids will also help.

If you have a cold, cycling outdoors in winter can aggravate dry air passages because of the low humidity associated with lower temperature. Wearing a face mask and drinking plenty of fluids should help alleviate this problem.

Should you stop training if you have a cold? Not necessarily. Unless there are complications, you should be able to maintain your cycling program. Simply drink more liquids, use a humidifier to increase available moisture, and take aspirin to relieve the aches and pains.

Don't ride with a fever

If muscle pains increase, ear infections develop, or a sore throat or colored nasal discharge appears, you should see a doctor and get antibiotics to fight the secondary bacterial infections. This is a time for rest, not training.

Should you ride with a fever? No. Fever is your body's defense mechanism against bacterial infections. It speeds up metabolism so that your body will produce more antibodies to kill invading germs. Fever may also be beneficial because many germs grow best at our normal temperature of 98.6 degrees. They don't multiply at higher temperatures. Fever is a guide that tells you your body is fighting bacterial infection and you're better off resting.

As soon as your temperature returns to normal, it's all right to resume cycling. You may be surprised, however, to discover how much endurance you have lost. Studies on endurance athletes show that after 10 days of not exercising because of a cold, they lost 10% of their endurance. The results may be even more devastating after colds accompanied by fever. A study conducted in Sweden showed that colds associated with muscle aches and pains kept athletes from regaining their full capabilities for more than three months. It took that long for certain chemicals necessary for energy production to return to normal levels in the muscles.

Once the worst symptoms of the cold subside, the question becomes how to recover. As long as the fever is gone, it's safe to continue cycling, taking care to ride within the limits of your energy and comfort and to stay warm. Gentle exercise actually tends to break up the congestion quicker than complete rest. But keep the pace down so as not to induce coughing.

Colds accompanied by fever and flu require more care. A period of convalescence — first complete rest, then a gradual return to a full schedule — is a must. As a rule of thumb, for each day of fever, take it easy for two days. For example, four days of fever and other symptoms would need eight days of recovery. Avoid hard cycling or you risk a relapse.

Bottles can carry more than water

Speaking of flu, don't overlook one good way to get it — from your water bottle. In fact, the custom of sharing water bottles with fellow cyclists can leave you (and your whole team) side-lined for weeks. Once you understand how susceptible you are to infectious diseases from contaminated water bottles, you'll see why it's important to keep your liquid containers clean.

Viruses that attack the gastrointestinal tract are spread via water. These diseases seem to follow a seasonal pattern, being most prevalent from May through October, a time that coincides with the height of the cycling season. Such diseases as pleurodynia (felt as pain in the chest) and aseptic meningitis are caused by water-spread viruses.

Some physicians believe that shared water bottles can also spread respiratory viruses like influenza. Saliva on the nozzle of the bottle may become airborne as water is squirted into the mouth. Those saliva droplets float into the back of the mouth where they are breathed into the throat and on to the nasal membranes. If germs are present, flu or respiratory infection can develop within days.

If several people on your cycling team are using the same kind of bottle, mark your bottles with your name and use only your own bottles at all times. Bottles must be routinely washed and disinfected. One good way is to drain the bottle, wash it in hot, soapy water, and then scour with a brush. Pay particular attention to the nozzle, lid, and inside bottom of the bottle.

If mold or other residue can't be removed by brushing, add clean sand or rice to the suds and vigorously shake the bottle until the abrasive materials loosen the residue. It's best to use light-colored bottles so you can see if residue is building up at the bottom. Dark bottles make it hard to tell.

After washing, soak the bottle for five minutes in a household bleach solution of one-half ounce (one tablespoon) bleach to one gallon of water. This will help to disinfect and sanitize. Rinse the bottle in cold water and drain. New bottles should also be disinfected as a precaution. (To help eliminate the offensive plastic taste of a new bottle, fill it with water mixed with a teaspoon of vinegar and let it stand for a few hours. Then rinse with cold water. The plastic taste will be neutralized.)

Like water bottles, water containers such as coolers can also invite trouble, since cyclists and trainers are likely to become impatient, take the lid off and dip bottles or cups in for a drink. This practice is most evident at feeding zones or at the finish of a race. Don't even reach in to get ice cubes, as this can contaminate the water with dirt, saliva, and sweat. Fill your bottle via the cooler spout or use a ladle to dip out water or ice.

Coolers, too, must be routinely washed and disinfected, with special attention paid to the spout. Flushing and swabbing helps prevent build-up of contaminants. To protect against bacteria and viruses, soak the containers for five minutes in the bleach solution, followed by a cold water rinse.

For added protection (or when traveling to foreign countries) consider using bottled water. Regulated by the Food and Drug Administration and the Environmental Protection Agency, bottled water offers you peace of mind. You'll know that what you're drinking is free of bacteria, contaminants, or other unwanted substances.

The water bottle is one of the most neglected pieces of cycling equipment. Remember, drink from only your own bottle at all times (avoid actually sucking on the nozzle so you won't contaminate the contents) and regularly disinfect and clean it.

Follow these simple tips and you'll go a long way toward preventing the spread of infectious disease.

Aspirin, tried and true

In this age of wonder drugs, when research laboratories and pharmaceutical houses are turning out a chemical cornucopia of relief for every ailment, the newest miracle drug may be the oldest — aspirin.

A standby of the medicine cabinet, aspirin is very effective for reducing pain and fever and as an anti-inflammatory agent. However, indiscriminant use of aspirin can cause allergic reactions, stomach irritation, prolonged bleeding, and even poisoning.

Aspirin belongs to a group of drugs known as salicylates. The active ingredient, salicylic acid, is found in the bark and leaves of willow and poplar trees and other plants. In ancient times, willow-bark tea was used to soothe pain. The drug was synthesized as acetylsalicylic, its current formulation, in the late 1800s. It came into widespread use at the turn of the century and today is perhaps the most popular nonprescription drug on the market.

There are three main properties of aspirin: to reduce fever (antipyretic), to stop pain (analgesic), and to control swelling (anti-inflammatory).

Asprin is helpful in controlling fever because of its effects on prostaglandins, the fatty acids produced by almost every cell in the body in response to mechanical, nerve, or chemical stimuli. Prostaglandins have been found in all brain cells and are important in the regulation of body temperature.

One prostaglandin is known to be a fever-causing agent. Its presence causes the hypothalamus, the temperature-control center of the brain, to reset the body temperature at a higher level. This higher setting causes the body mechanisms to conserve rather than to dissipate heat. Aspirin can reduce fever in two ways: by interfering with the formation of this specific prostaglandin, and by dilating the blood vessels of the skin, which increases heat loss.

It should be noted, however, that aspirin will not reduce a rise in body temperature caused by exercise. Physiologically elevated body temperature must be cooled by sweating and increased intake of fluids. Aspirin also increases sweating rates, so in hot weather aspirin use may lead to earlier and greater dehydration. Considering these adverse effects, I believe aspirin can predispose a cyclist to heat illness.

Everyone is familiar with the role aspirin plays in treating headaches, muscle soreness, strains, and other pains. Used as a painkiller, the standard dose is two 325 mg tablets taken four times a day. Aspirin's pain-killing effect is also related to prostaglandins. A specific prostaglandin, produced by inflamed tissues, increases the sensitivity of surrounding pain receptors. Again, aspirin inhibits prostaglandin formation, consequently reducing pain.

Asprin's ability to help control swelling and inflammation is not completely understood. However, many cyclists are aware of its effects in treating tendinitis, bursitis, and other conditions in which inflammation is a major problem. But the dosage taken to relieve pain won't have much effect on inflammation. Most physicians suggest 5-6 grams of aspirin per day if it is to be used as an anti-inflammatory agent. This comes out to 3-5 tablets taken four times a day — a dosage that should not be taken without the orders of a physician.

Beware of aspirin poisoning

While aspirin may be a wonder drug for the injured cyclist, it does have some major adverse effects. About 100,000 cases of serious, and sometimes fatal, aspirin poisoning occur each year.

Certain symptoms should alert you to the possibility of aspirin poisoning. Ringing in the ears is the most common first sign. Other indications are dizziness, headache, confusion, weakness, nausea, and faster or deeper breathing. If you have any of these symptoms, reduce or stop taking aspirin.

Some stomach damage occurs with even mild doses of aspirin and 40-70% of people taking it will exhibit some form of bleeding. Using buffered aspirin or taking milk along with aspirin can make it dissolve faster and so produce less irritation. Aspirin should never be taken with alcohol.

Aspirin has another effect on bleeding. As few as one to four tablets may delay the body's ability to clot blood. Under normal conditions this delay has little significance, but if you get injured while cycling, the delayed clotting could lead to extensive bleeding into damaged tissue. Menstruating women should also be aware of this delayed clotting action and discontinue aspirin use if bleeding becomes excessive.

Because aspirin is so commonly used, many cyclists no longer think of it as a drug. Nevertheless, it can have some serious side effects.

Acetaminophen and ibuprofen

Despite aspirin's well-recognized effectiveness, it has long had strong competition in the pain-relief market from acetaminophen (probably best known as Tylenol). Though usually a bit more expensive than aspirin, acetaminophen is much less likely to cause stomach irritation and gastrointestinal complaints. But though its pain-relieving properties are no less potent than aspirin, acetaminophen does little, if anything, to reduce inflammation.

Ibuprofen became available in the U.S. in 1974 as a prescription drug called Motrin, used to treat the inflammation accompanying arthritis. It was later found to be an effective pain reliever and is now available over the counter, under the brand names Advil and Nuprin. Ibuprofen works like aspirin in blocking the production of prostaglandins, and is also gentle on the stomach. It relieves pain and reduces inflammation.

Ibuprofen is by far the safest of the three drugs, but it still should not be taken by people allergic to aspirin. Most cyclists will find that ibuprofen is a good alternative to aspirin and acetaminophen for treating occasional aches and pains. Remember that it's most important to know the side effects of any drug you're taking and that the role of any drug should be limited and temporary.

Jet lag disrupts body rhythms

There are some situations that present extra health hazards for the hard-training cyclist. One of those is long-distance air travel and the resulting jet lag. For cycling vacationers or competitors who travel frequently, jet lag can be a real problem.

Most plants and animals, including man, have become synchronized with the 24-hour light-and-dark cycle. This is known as the circadian rhythm, from the Latin *circa dies*, meaning "about a day." Since our body rhythms are synchronized with the light-dark cycle, we sleep, work, and perform more effectively at certain times of the day than at others.

Body temperature, which drops very early in the morning or while we're sleeping, begins rising toward the afternoon. Blood pressure also fluctuates according to a 24-hour cycle, and hormonal functions are more efficient at certain times.

When the light-dark cycle is changed, as occurs when you cross several time zones while traveling, your body rhythms become desynchronized and you may experience problems with sleep, digestion, alertness, performance, recovery, and mood. Women may suffer menstrual pain or dysfunction.

Generally, the more time zones you cross, the worse you'll suffer from jet lag. For example, if you travel within one to two time zones, you may not notice any effect. Cross three to six zones and you're liable to notice some restlessness and perhaps a faster heartbeat. When you travel through 7 to 10 zones you may find yourself unable to fall asleep, or you may wake up at odd times. Cross more than 11 zones (from New York to Tokyo, for example), and the effect will be extremely noticeable as your body will be totally out of sync. Body temperatures will fluctuate wildly, eating schedules and appetite will be out of whack, and the hours when you're at peak performance level will change.

There are several things you can do to minimize the effects of extended air travel and the resulting changes in your circadian rhythm.

— For a few days before the trip, avoid riding excessive miles and don't be concerned about missing a day's training during traveling. A trip through several time zones is a workout in itself.

— Try to change your sleeping schedule before the trip. For instance, if you'll be traveling east, go to bed earlier and get up earlier for several days. If you'll be traveling west, stay up later and rise later. This way you adapt somewhat to the time schedule at your destination.

— Before the trip, learn about the environment you'll be entering. Prepare for the weather conditions, customs, food, transportation, etc. This may reduce some of the stress.

— During the flight do mild isometric exercises and walk around the cabin to relieve stiffness and boredom and to help lessen fatigue. Drink plenty of fluids to avoid dehydration, but stay away from alcohol or caffeinated beverages.

— During the first few days at your destination, resist the temptation to work out too hard. Take it easy or you may get worn down and increase your chances of getting sick.

In a recent study funded by the U.S. Department of Research, researchers discovered that careful manipulation of diet can minimize or reduce jet lag. The so-called "Anti Jet Lag Diet" was developed by Dr. Charles F. Ehret of the Argonne National Laboratory and has been used successfully by thousands of travelers, including former president Ronald Reagan.

ARGONNE ANTI JET LAG DIET			
Day 1	Day 2	Day 3	Day 4 (departure)
Feast	Fast	Feast	Fast (until...)
High-protein breakfast and lunch, high-carbohydrate supper	Low-calorie, low-carbohydrate meals (fruits, salads, light soups, toast, etc.)	Same menu as day 1	Same menu as day 2. If caffeine: westbound in a.m., eastbound 6-11 p.m. Break departure day fast at destination breakfast time.
Caffeinated beverages (coffee, tea, or cola drinks) between 3-5 p.m. only			Feast on a high-protein breakfast.

You can minimize the effects of jet lag by manipulating your diet in the days before your flight, preparing your body's clock for resetting.

The diet is designed to make use of food's effects on your body by alternating days of light and heavy meals. This continually empties and then refills the body's supply of glycogen, preparing the body's circadian rhythms for resetting.

The diet plan works like this:

Determine what your breakfast time will be on the day of arrival at your destination. Begin the diet three days before departure day.

On day one, feast — that is, eat heartily with a high-protein breakfast and lunch and a high-carbohydrate dinner. Drink coffee or caffeinated beverages only between 3 and 5 p.m.

On day two, fast — eat light meals of salads, light soups, fruits, and juices. Again take no coffee except between 3 and 5 p.m.

On day three, feast again.

On day four (your departure day), fast. If you drink coffee or other caffeinated beverages, take them in the morning when traveling west, or between 6 and 11 p.m. when traveling east. (When going west, you may fast for only half a day.) Drink no alcohol on the plane. If your flight is long enough, sleep until normal breakfast time at your destination, but no longer.

Break your final fast at breakfast time at your destination. Wake up and feast on a high-protein breakfast. Stay awake and active. Continue your day's meals according to normal meal times at your destination.

Feast days should focus on high-protein breakfast and lunch and high-carbohydrate dinners. High-protein foods such as steak, eggs, hamburgers, high-protein cereals, and green beans stimulate your body's active cycle. High-carbohydrate meals, on the other hand, stimulate the release of tryptophan, which causes drowsiness and sleep. Good choices of carbohydrates include spaghetti and other pastas (but no meatballs), potatoes, other starchy vegetables, and sweet desserts.

Fast days help deplete the liver's store of carbohydrates and prepare the body's clock for resetting. Suitable foods include fruit, light soups, broths, light salads, and unbuttered toast. On fast days, keep calories and carbohydrates to a minimum.

More information on the diet is available in the book *Overcoming Jet Lag,* by Charles F. Ehret and Lynne Waller Scanlon, published by Berkley Books, Post Office Box 690, Rockville Center, New York 11571. Or contact the Argonne National Laboratory, 9700 South Cass Avenue, Argonne, Illinois 60439.

Bacteria behind traveler's diarrhea

Another side-effect of travel can be just as debilitating as jet lag. It's known as "turista" and "Montezuma's revenge" in Mexico, but traveler's diarrhea is also common in Europe and the Mediterranean. Athletes visiting the Soviet Union have also suffered from it.

Many things can contribute to traveler's diarrhea, including changes in living habits, unusual food or drink, and viral and bacterial infections. But the primary cause is a bacteria known as E. coli (Escherichia coli), which stimulates the intestine to secrete too much fluid and electrolytes.

There are several things you can do to help prevent traveler's diarrhea. Try to avoid the bacteria. Peel fruits and stay away from leafy vegetables, unsanitary drinking water, and ice cubes that may have been prepared from unclean water.

A common over-the-counter medicine used to treat diarrhea is bismuth subsalicylate (better known as Pepto-Bismol). Its greatest benefit is that it is nearly nontoxic. It also seems to have some preventive effect. In a study in the early '80s, oral doses of two ounces taken several times a day reduced the incidence of diarrhea by 50%. Whether taking such large doses is worth the 50% chance of prevention is a personal decision. In any case, the compound is extremely safe.

If you do get traveler's diarrhea, go on a liquid diet that includes fruit juices high in potassium. As symptoms subside, add bland foods such as bananas, rice, toast, and eggs. Avoid dairy foods.

Some physicians prescribe an antibiotic called doxycycline (vibramycin) to treat diarrhea. Sometimes physicians prescribe Lomotil or Immodium for athletes. These can actually prolong the diarrhea by keeping the bacteria in the bowels.

Pollution is extra hard on athletes

Another problem you may encounter while visiting a new locale is air pollution. It may be a hazard in your regular training area as well.

Heavy atmospheric pollution is frequently the result of industrial discharge and automobile exhaust. In highly polluted environments your body is robbed of oxygen by the high level of carbon dioxide in the air and may also be irritated by the presence of other chemicals.

Imagine the situation in Los Angeles, the site of the '84 Olympics, where some of the highest levels of pollution in the world are recorded. According to experts from California's Air Resource Board, about 2,000 tons of total organic gasses, 1,300 tons of nitrogen oxides, 400 tons of sulfur oxides, and 1,500 tons of particulates fell on the Los Angeles area every day.

Athletes are at a special risk to airborne contaminants because they breathe more and faster during exercise. In addition, exercising athletes breath through their mouths, bypassing the scrubbing action of the nose.

Though there are many different chemicals that pollute our urban environments, carbon monoxide and ozone deserve special notice. Ozone is a gas that is diminishing in the stratosphere (where we need it for protection from ultraviolet radiation), but is increasing in many cities. It is the most toxic of all airborne contaminants and takes the highest toll on athletic performance. It can cause constriction of the lung passages, thus leading to labored breathing. Ozone is produced photochemically when sunlight strikes the hydrocarbons and nitrogen oxides that are released from auto exhaust pipes and smokestacks. Once created, it remains in the area for a long time.

Recent studies on athletes confirm that heavy exercise drastically increases ozone's toxic effects. Researchers in California found that in simulated ozone concentrations equivalent to an average-to-bad day (30 parts ozone per million parts of air) in Los Angeles, resting subjects experienced no impairment or discomfort. But almost half the subjects that were engaged in heavy exercise could not complete 60-minute tests, and all said they could not perform normally under these conditions. Many complained of wheezing, shortness of breath, headaches, and nausea.

Ozone: getting used to it won't help

Athletes in high ozone areas should consider training in the early morning or evening because pollution tends to increase rapidly after 8 a.m. to a peak early in the afternoon (about 1 p.m.) and then decrease to near background levels (below 10 parts per million) by 7 p.m.

No one can predict an athlete's sensitivity to ozone, but it has been shown that sensitivity diminishes with repeated exposure. This suggests that an adaptive response is taking place in the lungs as cells damaged by exposure are replaced by those more resistant. At the Institute of Environmental Stress, University of California, Santa Barbara, a study measured the effects of ozone exposure on young men for two hours each day for a week and found that their sensitivity was greatest on the second consecutive day of exposure. By the fifth day, they no longer responded to the ozone. In effect, they adapted. The greater the initial sensitivity, the longer it took for adaptation to occur.

Despite the adaptive response, you'd gain little by attempting to acclimate yourself to ozone pollution. Some athletes take a long time to adapt and others never adapt at all. Also, we don't know whether such adaptation is a healthy adaptation, as is acclimation to heat or altitude.

Carbon monoxide robs you of oxygen

Carbon monoxide is another form of air pollution found in large cities. It is emitted through car exhaust, industrial waste, and cigarette smoke. Its chief danger is that it squeezes oxygen out of the circulatory process. As carbon monoxide enters the blood stream via the lungs, it readily combines with the hemoglobin in the blood. Because it can combine with hemoglobin 200 times faster than oxygen does, it can cut severely into the body's oxygen supply. Even at low concentrations (5% or less of the air volume taken into the lungs), carbon monoxide has been shown to produce headaches, dizziness, confusion, and an increase in body temperature.

A study conducted on athletic performance after exposure to auto exhaust has ramifications for cyclists. A team of swimmers was driven around the Los Angeles area for an hour before a meet, while a control group remained at poolside. The control group did considerably better in competition. The implications for cycling are clear. More than one bike rider has found himself "gassed out" by cars, busses, and motorcycles during training or racing.

Here are some guidelines to help minimize the effects of air pollution:

— If possible, avoid cycling during the peak traffic periods, 6-9 a.m. and 4-8 p.m.
— During the winter, if you have a choice between morning and afternoon training, choose the afternoon. In the morning, wind speeds are generally light and pollutants are not as easily dispersed as they are late in the day.

— Avoid roads with heavy truck traffic.
— Stay as far to the right of the road as possible. A few feet can make a significant difference in exposure.

13 / Treating injuries

During the cycling season it's important not to lose valuable riding time to injuries, many of which can be easily prevented or treated.

Keep that crotch clean

That part of your anatomy on which everything in cycling hinges — your crotch — must be protected from skin-irritating friction. And I can't overemphasize the need for cleanliness in preventing pimple-like saddle sores and boils.

Boils and saddle sores may sound like minor problems, but races have been lost because of them. In 1987, pro rider Sean Kelly was leading the Tour of Spain when he was forced to withdraw because of a painful boil. He called it the biggest disappointment of his career.

Boils usually result from irritation to hair follicles. The predominant bacteria (staphylococcus) causes an infection and produces a pustule, which becomes enlarged, reddened, and hard. As inflammation and pressure increase, blood clots in the vessels deep in the core of the boil and tissue dies, which causes extreme pain when pressure is applied to the area.

Most boils will mature and rupture, emitting their contents. They should never be squeezed because this will force the infection into adjacent tissue. However, boils can be brought to maturity quicker by applying hot compresses. The sores should be treated with an antibiotic ointment. (In some extreme cases surgery may be necessary to open the boil.) After rupture, use an antibiotic ointment to prevent new boils on surrounding tissue.

The key to preventing minor irritations from developing into boils is to pay strict attention to hygiene. After every ride, clean your crotch immediately with soap and warm water. Dry well, then apply rubbing alcohol. Use the alcohol again before putting on your shorts for the next ride. Alcohol helps disinfect and toughen the skin.

You should wash your shorts with a mild soap after each use to remove sweat, grit, lubricant, etc. After the chamois has dried, you may want to apply lubricant to soften it. On leather chamois, you can use a product like Chamois Butt'r, A&D Ointment, Desitin, Noxzema, or your own formula. Several top cyclists in the professional peleton use a combination of Vaseline, lanolin, cod liver oil, and vitamin E.

Synthetic chamois dry faster than leather and don't hold as much moisture during rides. Synthetic chamois seem less likely to become stiff after repeated washings, but if needed, you can apply a product like Noxzema or A&D Ointment.

Road rash repair

Almost every cyclist will catch a case of "road rash" during his or her riding career. It happens in falls, when the skin is scraped away by the pavement. This exposes blood vessels, allows dirt and other foreign material to penetrate the skin, and increases the chance of infection. The scrape must be properly treated.

Begin by washing the wound with soap and water. Use a soft brush or sponge to get out *all* the grit. Apply hydrogen peroxide until the foaming subsides and then pat dry.

Next apply wound dressings to the affected area. Dressings help in several ways:

— Protecting the wound from germs and infection.
— Providing a moist environment to speed healing.
— Providing pressure to the wound, which reduces or limits swelling while increasing drainage.
— Protecting the wound from injury that might cause pain or disrupt the healing process.
— Preventing movement of the wounded area (especially arms and legs) that might interfere with healing.

Dressing can be a topical antibiotic ointment and non-stick covering such as Telfa, Adaptic, or Dermicel, or a self-adherent dressing such as Duo-Derm, Op Site, Second Skin, or Tegaderm. Both kinds keep the wound moist and protect it from germs.

Many cyclists use antibiotic ointments such as Bacitracin and Neosporin, which use a shotgun approach to the prevention of infection. They contain two or three different antibiotics, each effective against a different range of bacteria, to make sure nothing grows in the wound except skin.

According to a recent study, antibiotic ointments are preferable to traditional antiseptics like Mercurochrome, first-aid creams, and tincture of iodine, for effective wound healing. Wounds treated with double and triple antibiotic ointment healed in 8.8 to 9.2 days, faster than any other treatment. In comparison, wounds treated with iodine took 15.7 days to heal, and those treated with hydrogen peroxide took 14.3 days.

Antibiotic ointment should be covered with a non-stick dressing that is held in place by Bandnet, Surgiflex, or Stretch & Hold. These fishnet-like materials hold the dressing in place while still allowing full range of movement. Also, they hold the dressing without causing the excessive heat build-up experienced with tape. These products can be hard to find at your local drugstore, so you may have to buy them at a medical supply company. Dressings should be changed daily or oftener if needed.

The self-adherent, semipermeable dressings such as Second Skin keep the wound moist, which is important for skin growth. Several clinical studies have shown that when these products are applied to a clean wound and the dressings changed every 24 hours or as needed, most abrasions will heal in four to eight days. Once again, Bandnet, Surgiflex, or Stretch & Hold can be used to keep the dressing in place.

Remove dressings carefully so you don't injure the newly formed skin. You can rinse the wound with saline solution, but it's not necessary to remove all traces of the dressing material.

If your fall is particularly hard, you may want to keep swelling down by cooling the injured area as quickly as possible. Apply a cold compress to reduce swelling, minimize pain, and reduce bleeding under the skin, which causes bruising. For best results, cold must be applied before swelling starts. Since getting the ice on quickly makes a big difference, instant cold packs can be very helpful. These packs contain an inner bag of blue liquid that, when broken and mixed with the crystals, sets up a chemical reaction that produces instant cold.

The ice or cold pack should be applied to the wound after it is cleaned and dressed and held on with an elastic-wrap bandage. The bandage will provide compression that will also reduce the swelling.

These procedures should work in most cases, but occasionally infection does develop, usually in the first two to seven days. If you develop a fever, if the wound feels warm to the touch, or if the borders of the wound turn pinkish or red, consult your doctor as soon as possible.

There are a couple of precautions you can take to minimize road rash in a fall. First, always wear an undershirt when racing. That way, if you fall, your jersey will slide against the undershirt instead of your skin. Second, shave your legs (some riders shave their arms as well). This will help minimize the amount of skin lost because hair increases friction during sliding. Also, cleaning and bandaging a wound is easier without hair present, and the chance of infection is reduced.

Treat soft–tissue injuries with RICE

The most common injuries in cycling are to the muscle-tendon-ligament complex of the legs. These are called soft-tissue injuries and they are divided into two categories: direct and indirect. Direct injuries are usually the result of an accident, while indirect injuries occur mainly from repetitive overuse.

Direct injuries include contusions, strains, and sprains. A muscle contusion, commonly known as a bruise, often results from a fall. It happens when the muscle and associated tissue is crushed between a bone and the pavement. The skin is not broken, but there is pain, swelling, and discoloration.

A muscle strain occurs when there is a violent contraction or overstretching. Tendons, which connect muscle to bone, may also be injured. The type of stretch required to take a muscle and/or tendon past its normal range of motion usually results from a crash. You can reduce your chances of strains by keeping your muscles strong and flexible.

Immediately after a bruise or strain occurs, apply ice for 30-45 minutes. Repeat this treatment twice a day. Between icings, place a foam rubber pad on the injured muscle and hold it firmly in place with an elastic wrap. Elevate the leg. The idea is to discourage swelling and additional internal bleeding. Never apply heat.

The degree of pain, tenderness, swelling, and restricted movement varies with the severity of the contusion or strain. A black-and-blue bruise may appear within 24 hours in severe contusions and it may be painful to move. On the other hand, if you have a mild injury, you may be only slightly uncomfortable and have no problems moving around.

Continue ice therapy daily until the pain disappears and full range of motion returns. The hard blood mass (hematoma) associated with contusions will begin to soften in three to seven days. Stretching exercises can be done but not if they hurt. Do no forced movement and no hard riding. In the case of a severe contusion or strain that doesn't seem to respond to treatment, see a doctor to rule out the possibility of bone fracture and other internal injuries.

When can you resume training and racing? When the injured muscle feels almost free of symptoms and when you can move the limb without pain or stiffness. In some instances it may help to keep the muscle wrapped with an elastic bandage.

A sprain involves injury to a joint and ligaments (connectors of bone to bone). The signs of a sprain are rapid swelling, heat, and painful movement. Treatment is the same as for contusions and strains. If recovery is slow, you may have to immobilize the joint. You might need an x-ray to check for fracture.

There is often disagreement and confusion about whether to apply heat or cold to an injury. Most sportsmedicine experts say that acute injuries should always be treated with cold initially to control swelling and internal bleeding.

Cold quickly constricts blood vessels, which limits blood flow to the injured muscle, tendon, or ligament, thereby inhibiting hemorrhage. It also causes a slowing of metabolic processes within the tissue. This diminishes the need for nutrients that are carried by the blood. So less blood is required and that, too, helps limit the swelling.

As a general rule, rely on RICE — rest, ice, compression, and elevation — in the initial treatment of all acute cycling injuries.

Overuse injuries need rest

Indirect injuries include bursitis, tendinitis, tenosynovitis, and shin splints.

Bursitis is inflammation of a bursa, the pad-like sac or cavity found in connecting tissue near joints. A bursa contains synovial fluid, which reduces friction between tendon and bone or ligaments or between other structures where friction is likely. There are 18 bursae in the knee, the most common site of bursitis in cyclists. Injury can cause the inflammation, as can misuse — pushing a gear that's too big, pedaling from an incorrect position, riding without leg warmers on a cold day, etc.

The best treatment is rest and immobilization until the pain subsides. You may need to take analgesic drugs like aspirin to relieve the pain and use ice therapy to keep the swelling down. Heat and mild massage can be used in later stages of treatment. As soon as acute symptoms have let up, start easy riding to prevent the tissue from growing together. (Of course, it's essential to first correct any flaw in riding position that may have caused the problem in the first place.)

Tendinitis develops when a tendon (the fibrous tissue that attaches muscle to bone) becomes inflamed. The three most common types of tendinitis associated with repetitive activities like pedaling are patellar, Achilles, and popliteal.

Patellar tendinitis occurs to the tendon between the kneecap (patella) and the top front of the lower leg bone (tibia). This tendinitis is related to overuse of the quadriceps, the large muscles on the front of the thigh that are the power muscles of cycling. The quadriceps connects to the patellar tendon.

Achilles tendinitis occurs in the thick tendon that connects the calf muscle (gastrocnemius) to the heel bone (calcaneous). It can be caused by improper seat height or pedal action, or by early season rides in cold, wet weather.

Popliteal tendinitis results from the continuous locking and unlocking of the knee, which causes the popliteal tendon (rear and outside of the knee) to rub on the ligament that connects two of the leg bones (femur and fibula). This inflames the tendon, the ligament, and/or the bursae between them. The usual cause is a seat position that's too high.

The same treatment should be used for all these types of tendinitis: ice and rest. Then, after inflammation has subsided, apply heat and massage. Make sure to correct your riding position before you begin to train again.

Tenosynovitis is inflammation of a tendon sheath. The usual cause in cyclists is overuse, and two common locations are the Achilles tendons and peroneal tendons (on the back of the ankle). Tenosynovitis can be caused by improper cleat position or shoe placement, biomechanical foot defects, or poor pedaling technique. Heel lifts can be used to limit movement of the Achilles tendon, and the peroneal tendon can be wrapped or taped for support. Again, ice and rest are recommended treatment.

Shin splints can result from the sudden overuse of the flexor muscles located in the front of the lower leg. The irritation takes place at the base of the sheath that connects the two bones there. Contributing causes include faulty cleat position and arch problems. Treatment consists of icing for 20-30 minutes at a time along the entire front and inside edge of the shin. Arch supports and stretching may help. Take aspirin for relief of pain and inflammation. Healing usually takes a long time because of the limited blood supply to the area.

Those dreaded knee injuries

Injuries to the knee are perhaps the most feared in cycling, and with good reason — they are the most common cause of permanent disability in the sport. Knee problems can be caused by many things, including incorrect saddle height, improper cleat or foot position, cold weather, a direct blow in an accident, and using a gear that's too large, as well as inherited foot and leg abnormalities.

The knee is a simple hinge joint connecting the femur bone of the thigh to the tibia bone of the lower leg (see illustration). As many athletes discover, it's an unstable connection at best, depending on muscle, tendon, ligament, and cartilage for added sturdiness.

At the front of the knee joint are the quadriceps muscles, the kneecap (patella), and the patellar tendon. The underside of the patella is covered with a smooth, firm cartilage. The patella is important in straightening the knee, as it transfers the forces created by the quadriceps to the leg. It also helps protect the area from direct blows.

The back of the knee is supported by a group of ligaments referred to as the posterior capsule. The inner side is shored up by the medial collateral ligament, while the outer side is bolstered by the lateral collateral ligament.

The inside of the knee is stabilized by the anterior and posterior ligaments, which control front-to-back movements. Between the femur and tibia lie two cartilages that provide shock absorption as well as support. Finally, the knee is surrounded by synovial fluid and bursae for lubrication in the spaces between moving parts.

Chondromalacia

One of the most disabling knee problems in cycling is chondromalacia. This is often referred to as "runner's knee" because it's common among long-distance runners. Basically, the condition is due to poor tracking of the patella as it glides up and down in the groove between the femur and tibia during flexion and extension.

The term "chondromalacia" means disintegration of the patella and femoral cartilage surfaces. When the patella doesn't ride properly in its groove, the cartilage becomes rough and irregular. Symptoms start with deep knee pain and a grating or

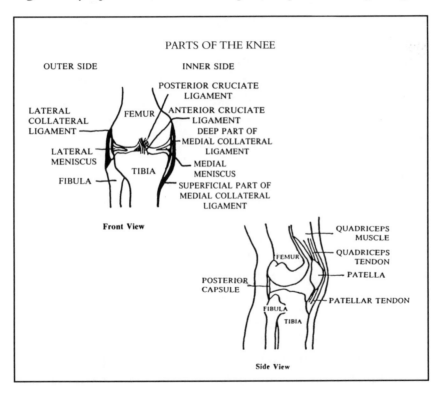

PARTS OF THE KNEE

OUTER SIDE   INNER SIDE

POSTERIOR CRUCIATE LIGAMENT

LATERAL COLLATERAL LIGAMENT

FEMUR

ANTERIOR CRUCIATE LIGAMENT

DEEP PART OF MEDIAL COLLATERAL LIGAMENT

LATERAL MENISCUS

TIBIA

MEDIAL MENISCUS

FIBULA

SUPERFICIAL PART OF MEDIAL COLLATERAL LIGAMENT

Front View

QUADRICEPS MUSCLE

QUADRICEPS TENDON

FEMUR

PATELLA

POSTERIOR CAPSULE

PATELLAR TENDON

FIBULA

TIBIA

Side View

Muscles, tendons, ligaments, and cartilage all help to maintain the strength and stability of the knee. But knee problems are among the more common injuries in cycling and can have many causes.

crunching sensation in the kneecap. The problem can seem to go away during cycling, only to return after the ride or later in the day.

Chondromalacia is difficult to treat, so it's important to recognize the early signs in order to prevent progression to chronic injury. Check your saddle height and foot position to be sure the pain isn't caused by incorrect adjustment. If your chondromalacia is caused by foot abnormalities, orthotics (custom supports worn in shoes) can often improve the condition.

Staying off the bike is essential. Treatment includes rest, aspirin, and application of ice to the knee for periods of 5-7 minutes. Once the pain is gone and the problem that caused it has been corrected, you can begin exercises to strengthen the quadriceps. Strong quads are important in the proper tracking of the patella. As a last resort, surgery is sometimes needed to treat chondromalacia. In the operation an arthroscope is used to shave off the inside of the kneecap. The opening into the joint is minimal in this procedure, and healing is usually very rapid.

Osgood-Schlatter's disease

Osgood-Schlatter's disease is a painful condition that strikes young cyclists. It is especially common in boys aged 10-14. The pain is felt in the front of and below the knee, and it can be aggravated by cycling. The powerful quadriceps attach to the patella and then to the patellar tendon, which is attached to the tibia. In rapidly growing youngsters, this area of the bone is the weakest. When the quadriceps contract and pull the patella and patellar tendon, the result is often inflammation and pain.

The condition can only be cured by growing out of it. Once the young person has reached the end of his or her major growth period, the problem should cease. However, in the interim, youngsters with Osgood-Schlatter's disease should not ride. If they do, bone fragmentation may occur on the tip of the tibia and surgery may be required. It may be difficult but necessary for some enthusiastic young riders to turn for several years to alternative sports like swimming.

Baker's cyst

Fluid accumulation behind the knee, which can occur when you have torn cartilage, arthritis, or other chronic problems, is a condition known as Baker's cyst. Usually it's painless, but the knee should be x-rayed to find the cause of the problem.

Kneecap dislocation

During a fall, your kneecap can become dislocated. The result is extreme pain and/or swelling, and the kneecap may actually look out of place. If you can't push it back into position, go to an emergency room for professional attention. Use ice to reduce swelling. Cyclists with a patella that chronically slips out should do strengthening exercises. Another option is surgery. A knee that tends to pop out at random may also lead to chondromalacia.

Knee ligament injuries

Mild injuries to ligaments, which attach bone to bone, can result from overstretching, overuse, improper position, or an abnormal twisting of the knee in an accident. Usually a little pain and inflammation are the only problems, and complete recovery can be expected after a week to 10 days of rest and application of ice.

Moderate ligament damage (partial tear) usually requires immobilization of the knee or other joint in a cast for three to six weeks. For a severely injured ligament (complete rupture), surgery is almost always required for proper repair.

Prostate is pressure sensitive

For male cyclists, there is one more area of potential injury to be concerned about. Fortunate indeed is the male rider who makes it through his cycling career without at least one bout of prostate problems.

The prostate's potential for trouble is directly related to its position in life. The walnut-sized gland surrounds the neck of the urinary bladder. Its primary function is the production of the fluid portion of semen.

You don't need much imagination to understand how infection or enlargement of the prostate can interfere with the relatively simple and comfortable act of cycling. Such enlargement or infection makes the prostate very susceptible to pressure directed between the anus and the scrotum. Cycling applies just such pressure, causing increasing discomfort.

Prostatitis (inflammation of the prostate) can be either acute or chronic. Acute prostatitis, usually caused by bacteria, is characterized by sudden fever, pain at the base of the penis, and painful and frequent urination. The prostate is swollen and tender. Sitting on a bicycle saddle or any other hard surface becomes a painful experience.

The condition should be treated with appropriate antibiotics. Bed rest and high fluid intake is recommended. (Dehydration can aggravate the symptoms.) If you're still able to ride your bike, be particularly careful to drink plenty of fluids during and after your rides.

Chronic prostatitis is usually a more difficult problem. Often no bacteria can be identified as the cause. Usually your doctor will prescribe a broad-spectrum antibiotic in the hope that it will alleviate the symptoms. Hot sitz baths will help reduce the tenderness. Some doctors, believing that emotions and stress play a role in chronic prostatitis, also will prescribe tranquilizers.

In advanced cases, rest, antibiotics, and hot baths will have to be continued until the inflammation has subsided. During this period, cycling will probably be out of the question and you may have to turn to running, swimming, or other exercise to maintain your fitness. (However, in some cases, cycling may be possible on one of the new recumbent ergometers that avoid putting pressure on the prostate.)

In mild cases of prostatitis, experiment with raising the height of your handlebars. This will require less forward lean on the saddle horn and minimize pressure on the tender gland. Installing upright handlebars or switching to a mountain bike will give you a more comfortable ride.

The choice of saddle can be crucial to maintaining or returning to cycling. A wider touring saddle will allow more weight to be supported by the buttocks. In some cases a saddle pad may be the only thing that will allow you to continue training.

If you're middle-aged, you may eventually develop a condition known as benign prostatic enlargement. This condition is presumed to be related to hormonal changes associated with aging. About 10% of men will have some form of prostate enlargement by age 40; by age 60, prostate enlargement is almost universal.

Benign enlargement is caused by an overgrowth of the prostate glands located adjacent to the urethra. This enlargment impinges on the urethra, narrowing the passageway of urine. Surgery is usually performed to eliminate the blockage. In such cases, you should follow strict guidelines from your doctor before resuming cycling.

14 / Taking care of your muscles

"My legs feel so heavy and sore I can't lift them. I'm going to stay in bed all day." You've probably uttered these words, or something like them, after your first race or hard ride of the season.

Everyone has sore muscles from time to time, usually within 48 hours after a hard effort. What causes this muscle soreness that makes walking down steps so difficult, and why does it last for days?

Many riders erroneously believe that such soreness comes from a build-up of lactic acid that can be decreased by cooling down after a ride. Although lactic acid is often responsible for soreness felt during and right after riding, research has shown that next-day soreness has other causes and should be handled differently.

Some soreness passes quickly

Muscle soreness is generally classified into two types: immediate and delayed. Both types come from cycling longer or harder than usual. The immediate type of soreness becomes apparent during or soon after riding and, although uncomfortable, usually passes quickly. Immediate muscle soreness is probably related to a temporary energy or metabolic imbalance that is corrected by rest and readjustment of body fluids and electrolytes. If cycling is intense enough to produce a lack of blood flow (ischemia), the resulting build-up of lactic acid causes more severe pain, which continues until the exercise is reduced or stopped and blood flow increases again.

The second type of muscle discomfort — delayed soreness — doesn't come or go as quickly. Instead, it appears 24-48 hours after strenuous riding and is usually accompanied by restriction of normal movement.

Three ideas about next-day soreness

There are currently three theories to explain this type of soreness. One of the oldest, Hough's Torn Tissue Hypothesis, is aptly named. It holds that an untrained muscle group can be damaged when subjected to long and hard work. Microscopic tears occur in the muscle fibers.

Another prominent theory is based on observations that the connective tissue of the muscle is irritated or torn by exercise. The connective tissue is the fibrous material that holds the muscle cells together and attaches them to bones. Hydroxyproline, a building block of connective tissue, has been found in the urine of subjects with delayed muscle soreness, suggesting that excessive physical activity may temporarily weaken the musculo-tendon unit.

Research by physiologist H. A. DeVries has led to a third theory — the muscle spasm theory of delayed soreness. According to this hypothesis, the sequence of events goes like this: The cyclist works out hard, causing a temporary lack of blood flow to the muscle. This ischemia causes pain in the nerve endings, probably activated by the release of a substance across the muscle membrane into the tissue fluid. The pain then sets off a reflex toxic muscle contraction (spasm). The spasm prolongs the deficient blood supply which, in turn, produces more pain.

Take steps to prevent sore muscles

Whatever the cause, there is still no medical cure for next-day muscle soreness. But there are a few basic preventive measures you can take.

Increase the frequency, intensity, and duration of your training gradually. Races and hard rides should not cover more than twice your average daily training mileage. Avoid sudden increases in distance or speed.

Also, do some mild physical activity after an exhausting ride or race. Such activity encourages blood flow, which assists in relieving the swelling in the muscle. Riding slowly on the days after a hard effort will help decrease the discomfort of delayed muscle soreness.

As a last resort, take two aspirin before riding and again afterward. An anti-inflammatory agent, aspirin may help to prevent the swelling that some people believe is connected to soreness. Aspirin appears to be safe for most people before exercise, but be careful because it promotes sweating and can cause dehydration. Be sure to drink plenty of fluids — about 8 ounces every 15-20 minutes during the ride. People with ulcers, kidney problems, or asthma should consult their doctor before trying this. (See chapter 12 for more about aspirin and its side effects.)

Passive stretches for active muscles

De Vries's research indicates that regular stretching can also be very effective in reducing muscle soreness. Measurements of muscle response to electrical stimulation show lower values after static stretching, and recovery from soreness seems to parallel lower values. What this suggests is that a cyclist who follows a regular stretching program may have less muscle soreness.

Use passive (non-bouncing) stretching. Hold each position for 30 or more seconds without bouncing. Relax for one minute, then stretch again for 30 seconds. The stretches illustrated here will take about 15-20 minutes.

Gastrocnemius stretch (back of leg): Place rear foot three to four feet from wall, keep upper body straight, slowly move hip forward until you feel the stretch in your straight leg. Do 30 seconds with each leg.

V-sit (hamstrings, lower legs, lower back): Sit with both legs straight and head in line with spine. Bend over straight from hips as far as possible — grabbing legs, ankles, or toes. Hold for 30 seconds. Repeat.

Shoulder stretch (upper back and shoulders): With hands on wall at shoulder height, walk backward three to four feet keeping feet about one foot apart. Straighten arms, bring spine toward floor, and lift buttocks. Hold for 30 seconds or longer.

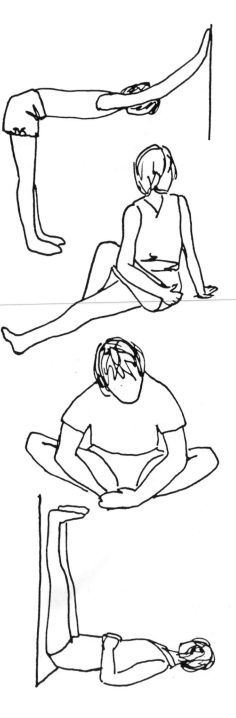

Trunk twister (back and hips): Sitting with right leg straight, place left foot flat at outside of right knee, reach over outside of left leg, turn head to look over left shoulder. Turn upper body but not hips. Hold 30 seconds. Reverse leg position and do other side for 30 seconds. Repeat twice on each side.

Yoga sit (groin and inner thigh): Sitting with knees bent and soles of feet together, draw the heels as close to the body as possible, push knees to the floor, hold 10 seconds, then relax. Repeat 10 times or perform for two minutes at your own pace.

L-stretch (improves circulation): Lie on floor with buttocks against wall and feet up. Hold one to five minutes.

J-stretch (lower back, buttocks, backs of legs): Lying on your back, lift your feet and roll your hips over your head. Keep your legs straight, lowering them until they touch the floor. (If this is too dificult, then bend your knees down to your head.) Use your hands to support your back. Hold for 30 seconds, relax, and repeat three times.

Tail leg stretch: Sit up with one leg bent directly behind you. Slowly lean back to stretch front of thigh. Hold for 30 seconds, repeat twice for each leg. Excellent stretch for quadriceps.

Low-back stretch (buttocks, lower back, and back of thighs): Lie on your back, pull one leg toward your chest, keeping your back and head on the floor. Hold for 30 seconds. Repeat twice with each leg.

Groin stretch (lower back and groin muscles): Lie on your back, bend knees, put the soles of your feet together, relax for 30 seconds.

Standing hang (lower back and hamstrings): From a standing position, bend over and let your body and arms hang (as if you were touching your toes). Hold for 10-30 seconds while body settles. Repeat twice.

Toe pointer (helps eliminate tightness in front of feet, ankles, knees, and thighs): Sit on feet, toes and ankles stretched backward. Do not allow toes to angle in and heels to go out. Hold for 30-60 seconds.

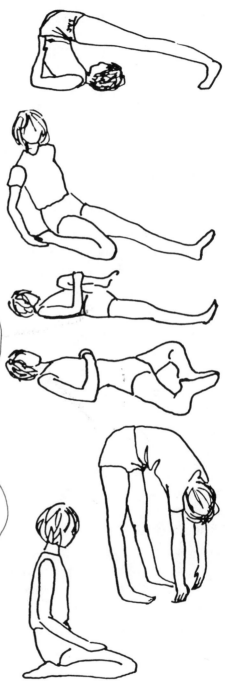

Massage helps muscles recover

Another thing that can help minimize muscle soreness is massage. Cyclists have used massage for a long time, and for good reason. It helps relieve pain, relax muscles, improve circulation, reduce fluid build-up, and increase flexibility. It aids flow through the lymphatic system and prevents blood stoppage in muscle capillaries, which causes swelling and tightness. It also improves the interchange of substances between the blood stream and tissue cells. Massage won't improve muscle tone or strength, but it's more effective than rest alone in helping a muscle recover from fatigue.

Professional bike racers use massage extensively. Massage plays a key role in each rider's recovery, enabling him to race or train hard day after day. Massage also has important psychological benefits — its soothing qualities are effective even when the rider's muscular fatigue is not that great.

If you are a coach or trainer, you may frequently serve as masseur for your riders. Here are some guidelines.

A cycling masseur's job is to help the rider maintain the best possible state of muscle health, flexibility, and vitality. To promote relaxation, the masseur should use a steady rhythm, which can be achieved by making the interval between each stroke the same. The rider should be on a table or bed at least 28 inches high, which allows the masseur to stand comfortably and cover a large area. A good masseur works with a swaying motion, which helps him produce rhythmical strokes and avoid back fatigue.

Massage should always be done on bare skin, and a lubricant should be used to prevent irritation and ensure smooth hand contact. Cold cream, baby oil, or lotions made specifically for massage all work well. Heavy oil isn't good because it leaves an excess on the skin. Some cyclists prefer a fine talcum powder, but this may not allow proper grasping of the muscles.

The room should be quiet and warm enough to keep the cyclist comfortable. When he's face up, a pillow should be placed under his head and a rolled towel under his knees. When he's lying face down, a pillow goes under his abdomen and a rolled towel under his ankles to prevent hyperextension of the foot. (There is no pillow under the head.)

As the masseur goes systematically about his work, he should guide conversation away from racing or training because such talk will not help the rider relax. He starts with light stroking, followed by deeper stroking, kneading, percussion, and friction. He should always be conscious of the cyclist's response to the pressures he is applying. Massage typically includes the following movements:

— Stroking (effleurage) is done toward the heart with the hands molded to the body. Pressure must be light. Hands should gently make and break contact with the skin. When done skillfully, this technique will produce a very soothing effect.

— Deeper stroking is used to assist the circulation and lymphatic systems, but the force must never be so great that it might irritate or injure the muscles. The idea is to stimulate flow of fluids to the nearest lymph gland (located in the neck, armpits, groin, and behind the knees). Deep pressure must always be directed toward the heart.

— Kneading means to grasp a muscle, apply and release pressure, then go to an adjacent area and repeat. Again, movements should be toward the heart and lymph glands. Kneading stimulates the large muscles and improves circulation.

— Percussion includes hitting with the side of the hand, tapping with the fingertips, and beating with the heel of the hand. None of this should be done to severely fatigued or injured muscles.

— Friction movements are made with the fingertips and thumbs to aid circulation around joints such as the knee, ankle, and wrist. When tissues are moved over the underlying structures in a circular motion, it helps loosen ligaments and tendons around the joint.

Five steps to a complete massage

During a massage, the rider should not turn over or move except when necessary. The masseur follows this procedure:

1. Start with the rider on his stomach and begin with the feet, using friction movements. Concentrate on the ball of the foot and the arch.
2. Move to the leg, using light stroking from the ankle to the buttock. Go back to the calf and hamstring and use deeper stroking and kneading. Spend about five minutes on the back of each leg.
3. Go on to the muscles of the buttock and lower back, which can be quite sore after pushing a big gear or climbing. Massage for about five minutes using stroking and kneading movements.
4. If the cyclist complains of upper body soreness, spend a few minutes stroking and kneading his back, neck, and shoulders to loosen the muscles there.
5. Now have the cyclist turn over. Apply light stroking from the top of the foot, over the knee, to the hip. Use friction around the kneecap. Pay particular attention to the thigh where the power muscles of pedaling are located. It's important to massage the entire thigh very well. Five minutes on each one should do it.

A complete massage after a hard effort will take at least 30 minutes. It should leave the cyclist feeling physically and psychologically improved. The best time for massage is in the evening, 60-90 minutes after dinner. This allows time for the food to be partially digested so more blood can be directed to the muscles.

There are times when massage should not be given, including during the presence of skin infection, acute inflammation, skin lesions, body temperatures over 100 degrees, muscle contusions, and circulatory disorders such as phlebitis, varicose veins, and thrombosis.

For more information, you may want to consult the book: Pozeznik, Roger. *Massage For Cyclists*. College Park, MD: Vitesse Press, 1995. A companion video is: *Massage For Athletes*. Kalamazoo, MI: Winning Touch Productions, 1997.

No masseur? Use self-massage

It would be ideal if each of us could have a massage after every hard training session or race, but most of us don't have a masseur standing by. The solution is self-massage. Spending four to five minutes a day on each leg will reduce fatigue and will help your muscles relax and recover.

Here are some tips on self-massage:

— Find a regular time to do massage every day. It may be just before bedtime or while you're watching TV after dinner. Be sure your skin is clean. You don't have to use massage oil, since it would simply have to be washed off later.
— Lie on the floor or on your bed. Put both legs up on the wall or a chair for three to five minutes. They don't have to be at a 90-degree angle, but they should be elevated at least 45 degrees. This will help drain the blood from your legs and give them a light feeling.

— Next sit up with your back against a wall, bedboard, or chair. Bend one leg and massage it completely, starting with the foot, ankle, calf muscles, knee, quadriceps, and hamstring muscles. Always work toward the heart with your movements since this is the direction you want the blood to flow. After about five minutes on one leg, switch to the other.

— After you've massaged both legs, you may want to return to areas that still feel tight or sore. However, stay away from any area that is very sore, since you may have some muscle damage and hard massage will only make it worse.

— Once you've finished massaging, elevate your legs again and relax for another three to five minutes.

Self-massage does take some time, but it's a worthwhile addition to your program, particularly during times of hard training and competition. Experiment to determine the stroking techniques, body positions, and time of day that are the most effective for you.

Analgesic balms for warm-up and relief

Stand in the staging area at any bicycle race and you'll smell the aroma of menthol in the air. The source of the scent is a tube of Musclor, Ben-Gay, Icy-Hot, or another of the dozens of similar products on the market.

Technically known as analgesics or counterirritants, these balms come in several forms — ointments, creams, or liniments. They're used in cycling to facilitate warm-up or to relieve sore muscles. They're called counterirritants because they produce a slight irritation of the skin and so create a sensation of warmth that can range from mild to intense.

Analgesics are made in varying strengths and different cyclists may react to them differently depending on the sensitivity of their skin. Putting a mild analgesic such as Icy-Hot on one cyclist will produce a hot sensation, while another rider whose skin is not as sensitive may notice only a slight warmth. Sensitivity may also vary from one part of the body to the other.

The most common ingredient in analgesics is methyl salicylate, which is found naturally in wintergreen oil. It is also manufactured synthetically. When applied to the skin, it causes redness and a feeling of warmth. Methyl salicylate is generally safe to use up to three or four times per day, but a cyclist who is sensitive to aspirin should carefully monitor methyl salicylate use, since the two compounds are related.

Menthol is the second most widely used ingredient in counterirritants. It's produced synthetically or extracted from peppermint oil. Menthol stimulates the nerves that perceive cold while depressing those that perceive pain. The effect is a sense of coolness, followed by a sense of warmth.

When a combination of menthol and methyl salicylate is applied, a mixed message of cold and warmth is sent to the brain, which has the effect of diminishing the perception of pain. That's why these products are used after a hard effort to lessen muscle soreness.

Do analgesics help in warming up? This has been a subject of debate for years. Recent studies at the University of California at San Diego measured the effectiveness of Ben-Gay as an aid in warming up before strenuous exercise. Two groups of runners were used in the study. One group applied Ben-Gay to their legs and warmed up. The other group warmed up without Ben-Gay. The runners then engaged in prolonged treadmill runs and recorded the amount of discomfort they were encountering at various times during the run.

The runners who warmed up with Ben-Gay ran with significantly greater comfort for a longer period of time. The researchers concluded that Ben-Gay aids warm-up and that a proper warm-up with Ben-Gay can help you exercise more comfortably for longer periods of time.

Take care when applying analgesics

The best way to get analgesic balm off your hands or to remove it from your legs after a race is with rubbing alcohol and an old towel.

Never apply analgesics to bruised or broken skin, since absorption into the body can sting. If you develop a rash, stop using the product and try a different one. Also, avoid using counterirritants near sensitive areas such as eyes, lips, and crotch.

When applying analgesics for cold-weather comfort, don't forget to roll up your cycling shorts to get the upper thigh and roll down your socks to get the Achilles tendon. It's also a good idea to apply some to the lower back if it's sore and to the arms if you're wearing a short-sleeve jersey. In cool, damp weather, use a product with an oil or petroleum-jelly base to help keep the rain off your legs and block the wind.

Have a coach or masseur apply analgesics to your legs. You don't want to start a race with analgesic on your hands as you're liable to rub your eyes or lips with it. One such experience will teach you not to apply it yourself.

For a long road race try this: Put some analgesic balm on one side of six-by-three-inch piece of cotton and then fold it over and wrap it in aluminum foil. Put it in your jersey pocket so that if it rains or the temperature drops, you can apply the analgesic to your legs or knees without getting it on your hands. Your coach or trainer can also put packets of counterirritants in your musette bag to be handed up in the feed zone.

Though counterirritants will aid in warm-up and help you recover from muscle soreness, they are not a replacement for a good warm-up on the bike. The sensation of warmth produced by the analgesic may make some cyclists think they are ready for racing when, in fact, their muscles may still be too tight for all-out exertion.

The painful stitch

Soreness isn't the only muscle problem associated with hard riding. You may have been among the many cyclists who have experienced muscle cramps or a "stitch" in the side that prevented you from staying with the pack or sprinting at the finish of a race. Cramps are painful, involuntary contractions of muscles, while a stitch is a sharp pain or spasm in the upper side of your abdomen.

The most widely accepted theory about the cause of a stitch is inadequate blood and oxygen supply to the muscles used in breathing — the diaphragm and the muscles between the ribs. When you're at rest, blood flows primarily to the liver, stomach, kidneys, spleen, and intestines. However, when you begin to ride hard, blood flow shifts from these organs to the large working muscles of the legs. Because the adjustment is not immediate, some muscles — in this case the respiratory muscles — are asked to meet the higher energy output without adequate blood flow. For example, at the beginning of hard effort in a race, you breathe deeper and faster and the demands on the respiratory muscles can be severe. The lack of blood flow may produce the stitch.

If you get a stitch during a race, try the following: Get in a safe place in the pack and stretch the arm on your affected side over your head. Blow out as hard as you can to empty air from your lungs or dig your fingers into the affected area of your abdomen and massage it.

Though these techniques sound fairly unscientific, they will work for many people. If they don't work for you, you'll be forced to slow down to decrease your metabolic demand, or you may have to stop riding completely.

If your stitch occurs regularly, it may be indicative of liver or gall bladder problems or a muscle pull, and you should seek medical advice.

Stretching and fluids can ease muscle cramps

Muscle cramps are caused by dehydration, electrolyte imbalance, or an inadequate supply of blood to the muscle. They are a direct result of fatigue and most often occur after rigorous and repeated muscular activity.

The most common variety are heat cramps, which occur during hot weather. The body relies on sweating to fight heat, and the resulting water loss causes a change in electrolyte and chemical balances in the body. Electrolytes such as potassium and sodium are responsible for generating the electrical activity involved in muscle contractions and for restoring the muscle to a resting state. You lose small amounts of electrolytes when you sweat and it may become difficult for your muscles to return to a non-contracting state.

If you feel a muscle cramping during a ride, you should forcefully stretch that muscle and its tendons. This will create tension on the tendons and activate sensitive nerve endings to inhibit further muscle contractions. This stretching technique is called reciprocal innervation. Every time you contract a muscle, the opposing muscle stretches to counterbalance it. If this were not the case, the muscles would contract against each other, as happens in an epileptic seizure.

If you have a cramp in your calf muscle, put the pedal in the six-o'clock position, drop the heel of the foot, and massage the affected area to increase blood flow to the muscle. When a cramp occurs in a thigh muscle, take that leg out of the pedal and with one hand pull the foot up behind you toward the seat. Once again, make sure you're in a safe place in the peloton or paceline before you perform these procedures.

To prevent or alleviate cramping, water replacement is crucial. You should also eat plenty of oranges, bananas, and fresh vegetables, as these foods contain high concentrations of electrolytes. Check your weight daily and make sure lost fluid is replaced and weight returned to within one pound of normal.

Good strength, endurance, flexibility, and racing fitness will help you avoid cramps and side stitches. As a final precaution, avoid heavy meals before competition. Finish your pre-race meal at least two hours before the start of the race.

15 / Dress for protection

It was the 14th stage of the 1988 Tour of Italy, described by many as the toughest in half a century. The riders had to traverse the 8,600-foot Gavia Pass in blinding rain and snow. Unlike most of the other riders, American pro Andy Hampsten had dressed for the winter conditions and so was able to make it to the finish several minutes ahead of his rivals. Though Hampsten had started the day more than a minute down on general classification, by the end of the stage he had taken the overall lead in the world's second-biggest stage race.

Hampsten said his choice of clothing had been crucial. "I put on my neoprene gloves because I knew that starting the climb I'd be fairly warm, but toward the top my hands would be too cold to put on my gloves. At the top of the climb I managed to get on a balaclava, a wool hat, and a plastic rain jacket. It was windy and I was pretty uncoordinated and clumsy, but the extra clothes absolutely saved me."

Though the outcome of a major international race may not hinge on it, your choice of clothing can be just as important to your safety and comfort.

Keep heat in, moisture out

Winter clothing should be selected with two goals in mind: to help you maintain a normal body temperature of 98.6 degrees, and to dissipate the excess heat and moisture you generate while cycling.

The combination of moisture, wind, and extreme cold can be devastating. Wind accelerates the loss of body heat and moisture conducts heat more than 30% faster than air. The greater the difference between body temperature and the temperature of the surrounding air, the faster the heat transfer. And the longer the ride, the greater the effect on comfort and safety.

Clothing insulation was once thought to be exclusively a function of thickness. Now we know that three other factors are also important: fiber reaction to moisture, heat conduction, and resistance to wind.

The higher the thermal conductivity of a fabric, the more it lets heat escape from the body. Cotton, for example, is much more heat conductive than some of the man-made materials. Evaporative ability is the rate at which a fabric dries once it's wet. The faster it dries, the sooner its insulating ability is restored. In dry conditions, however, it's mainly the thickness of a garment that determines its warmth. One inch of cotton can be as warm as one inch of down.

The basic function of fabric as insulation is to reduce air flow and trap heat. Every garment has some ability to trap air. On the average, fabrics trap about one-eighth inch of air between layers. Without taking into consideration the thickness of the material itself, four layers of fabric will provide one-half inch of insulation. However, if wind is able to penetrate the clothing, the insulation is less effective. This makes it important on windy days (and long downhills) for the outermost garment to be windproof.

New fabrics ward off water

Moisture — whether from sweat, rain, or snow — is a constant problem in cold weather because it reduces the fabrics' insulating ability. In fact, water conducts heat many times faster than air. This is why it's important to understand how the various fabrics in cycling clothing are affected by moisture.

For years, wool was the first choice of cyclists everywhere, and for good reasons. It's warm, it breathes, and it holds body heat even when wet. It can absorb up to 16% of its own weight in water without feeling damp or losing insulating ability. These advantages result from the many dead air spaces that form along the surfaces of the fuzzy fibers, and from their natural tendency to mat when wet.

Wool has some drawbacks, however, and in recent years has lost popularity. It's expensive, it can shrink or lose shape, and it's relatively heavy and bulky for the insulation it provides. Wool can also feel too warm on mild days or during hard efforts. New processing techniques are producing wool-blend and treated-wool fabrics that won't shrink or stretch and are easy to care for. However, these fabrics usually sacrifice some degree of natural wool's best qualities, such as insulating ability.

Cotton is excellent for summer but can be a hazard for winter use because of its high thermal conductivity (five times greater than some other fibers). Body heat, which must be conserved for safe cold-weather riding, leaves through cotton and escapes into the atmosphere. Cotton does absorbs moisture well, which suggests it would be good for removing perspiration, but wet cotton transfers heat up to 200 times faster than dry cotton, and it doesn't dry quickly. This makes cotton a poor choice for winter clothing.

Hydrofil nylon and polyester fibers both resist moisture and dry quickly. These fibers have some slight advantages for winter. They make you feel warmer because they don't conduct heat as readily. They also absorb more water before feeling wet, and they transport moisture away from the skin.

Another synthetic fabric, Lycra, allows perspiration to pass through quickly. It also reduces wind resistance by fitting like a second layer of skin. However, Lycra has little insulation ability, so wear it with other layers.

Acrylic was developed to provide the benefits of wool at a lower cost, but its fiber actually comes closer to nylon. Its insulation value comes from thickness and low fiber density. Acrylic can also wick moisture away from the skin.

Gore-Tex, AmFIB, ACTIVENT, and Ultrex are just a few of the new lightweight miracle fabrics that are waterproof, windproof, and breathable. These modern materials get their breathability from thousands of microscopic pores, which allow perspiration to escape but don't allow larger water particles to get in. To get the most from garments made of these materials, wear a minimum of other clothing underneath. This will prevent you from overheating and oversweating, which produces excess water vapor. Use convection currents to your advantage by ventilating as much as possible. These currents will remove excess vapor, as well as keep the body from overheating. The general rule is to close down sleeves, zippers, hoods, etc., just enough to prevent rain and wind from entering.

Therma Fleece and Thermax offer lightness, great breathability, and excellent insulation. These fabrics are also known for their water-hating (hydrophobic) qualites. Instead of absorbing moisture as cotton does, they wick moisture away from your body, keeping you dry and comfortable while you're cycling and sweating heavily. Wickability makes polypropylene and Thermax the ideal fabrics to wear next to your skin. Some athletes add a second, heavier-weight layer of the same fabric. This way they get insulation without weight, and take full advantage of the material's wicking ability. Follow this up with a windproof, breathable shell and you have the perfect cold-weather clothing system.

Polypropylene garments do require special care, however. Washing by hand will reduce pilling. Polypropylene will melt in very hot water or in a dryer, but since it air-dries very quickly, it should not need machine drying. New fabrics such as Thermax (made by DuPont) and Phin Tech (Pearl Izumi) hold up better under washing and drying.

In summer play it light and loose

Your choice of warm-weather riding apparel, while not a matter of life and death, can also have great impact on riding comfort. When choosing summer wear, your two main considerations should be color and type of fabric.

In general, light colors feel cooler than dark colors when worn in sunlight. White is the coolest of all. So why is it that each season there are team jerseys featuring dark colors? There are practical advantages to dark colors, such as covering ability (the same thin, porous fabric in a lighter color may let the skin show through) and the tendency to hide dirt and stains. But the fact remains that a black jersey will absorb up to 95% of the energy of sunlight, while a white jersey may absorb as little as 30%. The value for an intermediate hue like blue or green is 50%.

Fabric texture is as important as color. A loosely woven material is better than a tight weave because it will let the air through to help evaporate moisture and cool the body. The new materials such as Fieldsensor and Cool-Max are excellent because they are light and they stretch for a comfortable fit. Also, moisture passes through them quickly and they won't become heavy with rain or sweat.

Use gloves to pad and protect

Another important clothing item to consider is a pair of cycling gloves. Here are several good reasons for wearing gloves:

— to help prevent hand injury caused by road shock and vibration
— to protect your hands in a fall
— to shield your hands while cleaning debris from tires
— to improve handlebar grip, especially in wet weather
— to provide protection and comfort during cold-weather cycling.

Fit is the most important factor in selecting gloves. Always try gloves on before buying. The shape of the palm pad should feel comfortable when you grasp the handlebars. Finger holes should be snug but not tight. Remember that a leather glove will stretch over time, so a new pair should fit snugly.

The thickness of the palm covering is also important, as it protects the nerves in your hands. Road shocks, vibrations, and continued pressure on these nerves contribute to the common cycling injury known as ulnar neuropathy or "handlebar palsy." The ulnar nerve is the major nerve of the lower arm. It runs along the inside of the arm before entering the hand a short distance above the wrist on the palm side. Extreme stress on the ulnar nerve causes hand numbness, weakness in grip, and loss of muscular control in the fourth and fifth fingers.

Every time you ride, road vibration and the impact of road shocks are transmitted through the bicycle to your body. If ignored, continued pressure and vibration in the palms can lead to permanent nerve damage. Adjusting your handlebars to distribute your weight better, changing your hand position frequently, and using handlebar padding can decrease pain and discomfort or eliminate the problem entirely. Properly padded gloves can also help.

Gel gloves absorb road shock

In the last few years several companies have introduced a new type of glove that incorporates viscoelastic polymers or "gels" into the padding. These gels add an extra protective layer of life-like synthetic tissue that absorbs handlebar pressure. The gels dampen the road shocks and vibrations that are transferred through the handlebars to the hands, elbows, and shoulders. Also, unlike foam padding, gels don't compact over time and lose their ability to lessen road shock.

A recent study compared the ability of different cycling gloves to absorb road shock. Cyclists were asked to ride on rollers with instruments to measure shock attached to their handlebar stems and to the back of their left hands near the wrist. A half-round wooden dowel was attached to the front roller to produce road shock of the amplitudes and frequencies expected on the road. The cyclists rode the rollers barehanded for several minutes and then repeated the procedure wearing various types of gloves. Data on the peak shock at the wrist and stem were recorded.

The results indicate that, compared to leather gloves and foam-padded gloves, gel gloves provide more cushioning and protection from road shock. In this study, the natural padding of the hands alone provided an average reduction in shock between the bar and wrist of 24%. When gel gloves were worn, this decrease in shock improved to 39%. These findings are important to any cyclist who has experienced hand numbness and needs improved padding to cushion road shock.

Proper care will extend the life of your cycling glove. Always remove a glove by grasping the wrist and peeling the glove down your hand so that it comes off inside-out. Removing by tugging the fingers will break the threads and stretch the glove.

Gloves should be washed occasionally in mild soap, but don't dry leather gloves in the dryer or direct sunlight, because they will shrink.

When selecting winter gloves, make sure they flex easily and aren't too tight. A glove with a slightly loose fit allows some air circulation and will be warmest. Until recently, many warm gloves were very bulky, making it difficult to properly feel the handlebars. Fortunately, new synthetic fibers such as 3M's Thinsulate and DuPont's Thermolite have allowed manufacturers to produce gloves that aren't as bulky but still provide enough warmth to protect your hands.

Take time to choose the right shoe

Proper cycling gloves are important and it's worth investing some time and money in finding a suitable pair. You should also spend some time choosing another important piece of equipment — cycling shoes.

Each year we see more and more major athletic shoe manufacturers entering the cycling market. Each company claims that new research has led to improved performance. Newer and better materials have been incorporated into their product, they say, to produce the "ideal" cycling shoe.

Does this mean you no longer have to spend much time finding the proper cycling shoe? Absolutely not. In fact, the opposite is true. Having such a broad range of shoes (and pedal systems) means taking extra care with your shoe investment.

The first step is to realize that just because your favorite pro cyclist wears a particular type of shoe doesn't mean it's the best for you. Each person and each pair of feet have different requirements.

Don't buy the first pair you try on — be prepared to spend some time shopping around. Bring along the socks you normally wear so that you'll get a true fit when sampling shoes. Try the shoes on late in the day, as feet tend to swell during the day and this will better duplicate the size of your foot after an hour or more of cycling.

Once you have a shoe on, stand up and put weight on the sole. If the shoe feels as comfortable as your everyday street shoes, it's too big! Try another pair a half-size or so smaller to get a snug fit. Remember, leather shoes will stretch and conform to your feet after several riding sessions. Nylon mesh, on the other hand, doesn't stretch at all.

The sole should be contoured to the shape of your foot and should hug your foot snugly. Some soles will fit better depending on whether you're flat-footed or have a high arch. If you're flat-footed look for a shoe with minimum curvature of the sole; cyclists with high arches will feel better in a shoe with a high heel.

Today the soles of most cycling shoes are made of nylon, lexan, or composite material. The soles are stiff to ensure that the force of pedaling will be directed into the pedals. However, stiff soles can also lead to "hot feet" in long road races. This is particularly true when races are held on rough roads.

If you experience hot feet — a numbness or burning sensation in the ball of the foot — you have several options for treatment. First, check to make sure the toebox of the shoe is wide enough for your foot. You may also use a thin replacement insole in your shoes to reduce pressure and create a more even distribution of pressure on the pedal. Replacement insoles are available at most sporting goods or drug stores and should be worn when buying shoes.

If you still have problems, you might try using a leather-soled shoe with an insole, since leather absorbs road shock better than nylon or lexan. Lastly, you might consider using one of the new clipless pedal systems. They eliminate the need for toestraps, which can constrict blood flow to the forefoot.

The shoe closure you choose can also affect your cycling comfort. Closures can be Velcro, laces, or a combination of both. Velcro closures are popular among triathletes because they make the shoes easy to get in and out of during transitions from swim to bike and from bike to run. Another advantage of Velcro is that tension can be adjusted during long rides; you can loosen the closure if your foot swells or tighten it for the final sprint. The cyclist who likes a snugger fit and uniform tension across the top of the foot may be happier with laces. However, laces cannot be adjusted during the ride. A combination of lace and Velcro closures, used on several new models of shoes, may be the best compromise for ensuring fit and comfort.

Get reinforced shoes for clipless pedals

If you're one of the majority of cyclists who now use clipless pedals, you should buy a shoe with a reinforced upper. Make sure the shoe has a built-in strap that is anchored to the sole and then connected to the lace or Velcro closure system. These straps are necessary to resist the upward pull on each pedal stroke. Without this additional support, the uppers will stretch and may even separate from the sole. Several companies now sell add-on external Velcro straps that can be put around the sole and upper to support the shoe.

Make sure the cycling shoes you buy have heel counters — hard or premolded sections that strengthen the heel of the shoe. Heel counters stabilize your heel, reduce heel drift, provide a better fit around your heel, and prevent your foot from rolling inward (pronating) during the power phase of the cycling stroke. If you use orthotics while riding, you'll get better performance from a shoe with a stiff sole and firm heel counter. Heel counters are even more important in shoes used with clipless pedal systems. As well as providing better rear foot support, they help preserve the uppers.

Replace your cycling shoes if the uppers or heel counters wear out and stop giving proper support. If you do a fair amount of riding in wet weather, you'll find that a nylon mesh shoe with a synthetic sole will hold up better than a shoe with leather soles and uppers.

Winter riding can be particularly hard on your cycling shoes, as well as on your feet. It's better to wear insulated shoe covers over your shoes than to try and wear heavy socks, which overstretch the shoes. Some European cycling shoe manufacturers also sell fleece-lined shoes with water-resistant liners for improved comfort and performance during winter cycling.

Finally, check your cleats every few months and replace them when the cleats or the fastening bolts become worn. Also, check your cleat alignment after a crash, since an out-of-position cleat can cause knee, ankle, or foot problems.

Sunglasses block harmful rays

In recent years we've seen a huge increase in the number of cyclists who wear sunglasses while riding. They have become the rule rather than the exception — and for good reason.

The primary function of sunglasses is to protect your eyes against glare. For the best protection, they should block out 75-95% of visible light in bright sun and 35-50% on a cloudy day. Before you go out and buy a pair, exorbitant prices aside, you should understand a few basics about sunglasses.

It's the unseen wavelengths, both longer and shorter than visible light, that can damage your eyes. On a long ride, particularly in the mountains where thinner air filters less light, at least 85% of the ultraviolet (short wavelength) rays should be removed. There is evidence that overexposure to ultraviolet radiation can cause brown (sunshine) cataracts — the gradual accumulation of pigment on the eye's lens, similar to a freckle on the skin. At the least, such exposure certainly causes irritation and inflammation.

Ultraviolet light inhibitors can be incorporated into glass, plastic, photochromic, or polarizing lenses, and are impossible to detect by looking at the lenses. Check the tag to see how much ultraviolet light the lenses absorb. The higher the better, right up to 100%. Don't be misled just because a tag says "absorbs UV light." Look for a stated percentage.

Infrared (long wavelength) radiation is less damaging, but after you've been in the sun for an extended period it can cause a raw, burning sensation. It may also cause eye fatigue and leave you tired and irritable. Look for sunglasses that filter out most infrared rays as well. Some glasses filter 100% of both infrared and ultraviolet radiation.

The darkness of the lens is also important because it filters out visible light and glare. Visible light may be less damaging than light you can't see but it, too, can leave you squinting as you ride. The degree of darkness you should select depends on the situations in which you most often use sunglasses, but don't go too dark or you might not be able to see. For example, glasses that are used to protect skiers from snow glare are often too dark to ride in. Wearing darkly tinted glasses that have no ultraviolet light protection can be worse than wearing no sunglasses at all, because the pupils of the eyes widen behind the dark lenses, allowing more harmful rays to enter.

In terms of color, many opticians recommend gray tints because they soften all colors but eliminate none. Amber/brown is also very popular. Photochromic lenses, which darken as the light increases, will cover the large range of light conditions found in long road races or training rides. These lenses are available in both plastic and glass and come in various density ranges.

Your risk of eye damage is proportional to the length and intensity of exposure to the sun. How much protection you need and when you need it depends on what you do and how long you'll be outside. Make sure you wear glasses if you're going out on a long ride or spending a long time in a bright environment. Remember, ultraviolet light radiation is greatest at high altitude.

In addition to filtering ultraviolet and infrared light, sunglasses protect your eyes from dust, debris, and pollutants. Sunglasses are especially helpful for extended rides, particularly while riding in dry environments or near the beach, since sand can be abrasive to the eyes.

You may be one of many cyclists who've experienced "dry-eye syndrome." After several consecutive days of long rides, such as in a stage race, you may find that your eyes feel dusty and dry. This can be controlled by using wraparound sunglasses or goggles, which keep out the wind. I also recommend using a commercial wetting solution as an eye lubricant.

Before you buy your next pair of sunglasses, examine them carefully to see that they meet all the necessary criteria. Remember that, though good sunglasses are sold in stores and through the mail, so is a lot of junk. Trade names (and the fact that a well-known cyclist wears a particular brand) do not assure absorption level. Nor does price assure quality, because the frame can cost more than the lenses. The bottom line is that a good pair of sunglasses will cost you between $40 and $150.

Check the distortion in the sunglasses you buy. Hold them at arm's length and look through them at a light source. The image should be clear across the whole lens.

As for durability, note that though sunglasses rarely break while you're riding, even the best glass ones can shatter in a crash. Polycarbonate lenses, though, are almost unbreakable. You may have seen advertisements that demonstrate the indestructibility of these lenses. Even when bullets are shot at them they will split in half, but they won't splinter. They're also lighter and won't fog up as readily as glass. It should be noted, though, that plastic lenses scratch and aren't always as optically accurate as glass.

Consider durability and fit

Choose frames made of nylon or plastic because they are lighter, more durable, and safer than the old metal ones. They will also be safer if you crash and hit your head, because they won't shatter into sharp fragments.

Finally, pay attention to fit. Select frames that fit properly and don't hesitate to have them adjusted.

Taking care of your eyes will go a long way toward keeping you safe and injury-free.

16 / Drugs and ergogenic aids

Athletes often feel a tremendous amount of pressure to perform to their maximum. Some of that pressure comes from within, but it's also heaped on them by friends, family, teammates, coaches, and fans. So it's no surprise that top-level athletes are tempted to use drugs to gain an advantage over their opponents. Coaches and trainers have even been known to encourage such drug use, and to provide the substances.

Two recent events, the use of EPO and anabolic steroids, illustrate how drugs have infiltrated many sports. In the last few years, there have been many anecdotal reports and complaints by fellow athletes and coaches that athletes are taking a new hormone erythropoietin (EPO). EPO is a recombinant form of a hormone that increases the amount of red blood cells in the circulation, which has been shown to increase the oxygen carrying capacity of an athlete and thus produce more work.

During the 1996 Olympics, several athletes in events such as track and field and weight lifting were found to be taking anabolic steroids to help build muscle mass for increased power and strength. EPO and anabolic steroids will be discussed in greater detail later in this chapter.

Why drug control?

The misuse of drugs has resulted in deaths at all levels of cycling, yet some people question the need for doping control. They say, "Why shouldn't a rider have the choice of any method of training or any drug despite its potential health danger? If he dies attempting to excel, it's his responsibility."

One reply is that the use of drugs contravenes a basic characteristic of sport: the matching of strength and skill based on the natural capabilities of the athletes. But beyond this ideal, there are several practical considerations. For example, the use of some drugs, such as amphetamines, can cause aggression and loss of judgment. A rider taking amphetamines may be a danger to other cyclists, to spectators, and to officials. Also, it's natural for young riders to emulate the established heroes of the sport. If leading cyclists are allowed to use drugs in competition, many others would be sure to follow suit.

Since 1960 there has been an ongoing crackdown on the problem of drug use by cyclists, and new substances are continually being added to the list of those drugs banned from the sport. Still, each season there are positive findings in post-race urine tests.

Medical controls are now part of all major national and international competitions. Every cyclist, coach, manager, and team physician should be familiar with how dope testing is done.

How drug testing works

The first four finishers and at least two riders selected at random are required to report to medical control to submit urine samples after a race. (In stage races, samples must be supplied by the first two finishers in the stage, the leader on general classification, and two riders picked at random. After time trial stages the four fastest riders must report.)

If you're selected for medical control, an official will notify you soon after the event by presenting you with a card. You must sign a copy of the card to indicate that you have been notified. You then have 60 minutes to report.

If you're riding in a second event or are delayed for some reason, a representative from your team should tell medical control where you are. If you don't report, you face immediate disqualification from the event and suspension of your racing license for one year.

Only authorized personnel are allowed in the medical control area. This group includes the supervising physician, race officials, and male and female chaperones. You should bring your team physician or manager with you when you report.

After signing several forms, you will be given two 50-milliliter bottles and one 150-ml receptacle. You will be escorted to the laboratory where you must make yourself naked from the middle of your back to your knees in order to prove that you have no concealed tubes or containers. You must also roll up your sleeves to make concealment impossible.

Collect your urine in the large receptacle and divide it between the small ones, which must each contain 35-50 ml. An official will close the bottles by applying either a sealing wax or lead seal directly to the stopper. You may also affix your own seal, if you have one. For example, two-time Tour de France winner Laurent Fignon seals the containers with the crest of his wife, who is related to French nobility. Finally, a form is signed by all concerned to verify that the full procedure has been carried out properly.

If you're unable to urinate right away, you'll be kept in the facility for as long as it takes. There is no time limit. Should the doctor permit you to leave for some reason, such as an interview with the press, an official will stay with you until you're finally able to give a sample.

The collected urine is then shipped to the nearest approved lab for tests to determine whether any drugs are present. Usually the results are ready in 12 to 24 hours.

If the test on the first sample is positive and the athlete appeals the finding, the urine in the second bottle will be tested in the presence of an expert appointed by the event's host country. This person must be there when the seal on the bottle is broken and the contents are analyzed. Riders may be represented by their own physicians.

The rules and penalties for drug violations are constantly being updated and are beyond the scope of this book. But, as a recent example, amateur U.S. cyclists faced these penalties:

— Blood boosting or use of prohibited steroid, diuretic, probenecid, or related compounds: two years' suspension.
— Use of a prohibited stimulant, narcotic, or analgesic: six months' suspension. The penalty for first-offense use of narcotic, analgesic, or stimulant may be reduced under the following conditions: the substance was an ingredient in a product the use of which the rider declared in writing at the time of testing, the product was prescribed by a physician or was legally obtained over the counter, the product was not used in abnormally high quantities, the lab results do not support the conclusion that the product enhanced performance.

It's not only the rider who faces penalties. Any U.S. Cycling Federation official, coach, or rider who provides a rider with a prohibited substance or facilitates a prohibited practice such as blood boosting, or who encourages the use of such a substance or practice is subject to the same penalties as the rider. Anyone who tries to alter, falsify, or subvert medical controls also faces suspension.

Current information on the drug policy and education program of the U.S. Olympic Committee can be found on the web at http://www.olympic-usa.org.

Don't take it unless you know what's in it

One common misapprehension about drug testing is that nothing is safe to take. This is simply not true. For example, aspirin and some other anti-inflammatory drugs are acceptable. In general, most medical conditions requiring drug therapy can be treated by a non-banned substance. In fact, even serious problems such as acute asthma can be treated by substituting safe drugs for stimulants like adrenalin and ephedrine.

A simple rule to follow is that you can put anything you want into your mouth, as long as it's food. If it's anything but food, find out what's in it. I'm amazed at what medications, drugs, supplements, and potions cyclists will put in their body without first knowing what they're taking.

Read the list of ingredients to be sure you're not ingesting anything you shouldn't. Banned substances may be found in the most seemingly innocuous agents. For example, Stay Trim gum contains phenylpropanolamine, a banned stimulant. Midol, a familiar over-the-counter medication used to relieve menstrual cramps, contains cinnamedrine, which breaks down into ephedrine, a banned substance. A large dose of Midol taken just before a race could result in a positive drug test. To complicate matters further, cinnamedrine is found in Original Formula Midol and Maximum Strength Midol, but not in Midol PMS or Midol 200.

I'm often asked why it is that, in recent years, more athletes seem to be getting caught by drug testing even though testing has been done for over 25 years. The answer is accuracy. Before 1983, the most commonly used tests were crude so-called "sink tests" (and, unfortunately, some countries still rely on them). With sink tests, some samples were tested while the rest were poured down the sink. And there was no guarantee of accuracy even for the few samples that were tested.

The first truly accurate tests were conducted at the 1983 Pan American Games in Venezuela using a method developed by Dr. Manfred Donnke of West Germany. His tests used two sophisticated lab techniques: gas chromotography, which separates the components in the urine samples; and mass spectrometry, which identifies the molecular weight of each of the separated compounds. The test can identify substances to the level of one part per billion. The same testing procedures were used at the 1984 Olympic Games, and all testing by the U.S. Olympic Committee is currently done the same way.

The latest list of substances banned by the USOC contains more than 235 products and continues to grow. This underscores the cyclist's need to be informed and up-to-date. If you have any questions about a substance, call the toll-free USOC Drug Control Hotline at 800-233-0393.

Ergogenic aids: benefits and side effects

Athletes have always sought a magical substance or training aid to give them a competitive advantage over their opponents. When special substances or devices are employed to improve performance, the substances are known as ergogenic (work-enhancing) aids. Most ergogenic aids can be grouped into five categories: nutritional (vitamins, carbohydrate or bicarbonate loading), pharmacological (caffeine, growth hormones, steroids, probenecid), physiological (oxygen, blood boosting), psychological (hypnosis, imagery training), and mechanical (aerodynamics, new techniques). Here is a roundup of some of the pharmacological and physiological ergogenic aids currently in fashion.

Steroids

One of the most disturbing recent trends in sports is an increase in illegal steroid use among athletes.

Anabolic steroids are synthetic derivatives of the natural male steroid hormone, testosterone. Anabolic refers to hormones that promote tissue growth, increase muscle mass, and increase hemoglobin concentration without prompting concurrent development of the secondary male sexual characteristics such as abnormal hair growth. These hormones work by stimulating protein synthesis.

Doctors use anabolic steroids to treat such diverse health problems as osteoporosis, anorexia nervosa, breast cancer, and anemia. Steroids also promote healing of severe burns, fractures, surgery, infectious diseases, or general run-down condition, all of which occur in people of both sexes and all ages.

For athletic training, however, anabolic steroids have a different use. Research indicates that high doses of anabolic steroids combined with heavy weight training will result in an increase in body weight and muscle size — desirable changes for some athletes. (The weight gain is the result of an increase in both body water and lean body mass.) Testosterone also increases the level of glycogen in muscles. Glycogen is the primary fuel of working muscles, so the net effect is an increase in endurance.

Because of the possible increases in strength, you can see why sprinters and kilometer riders would use anabolic steroids. But why are road cyclists testing positive for them?

The answer lies in the effect steroids have on the blood. Steroids can increase aerobic capacity by increasing the blood's ability to deliver oxygen to working muscles. Taken in large doses over a period of several weeks, anabolic steroids increase absolute red cell mass. At first there may be no change in the hemoglobin concentration, but the actual blood volume may increase more than 15% above normal. Once steroid use is discontinued, the extra plasma volume is swiftly reduced to pretreatment level, leaving the increased red blood cell mass.

The increased level of red blood cells and elevated hemoglobin concentration may last for several weeks.

Because steroids increase aerobic potential and help athletes endure more work, it's no wonder stage racers take them. But there are many dangerous side effects associated with steroid use. Excessive water retention occurs with all these drugs and accounts for at least a portion of the desired weight gain. Increased secretion by the sebaceous glands can lead to acne, especially in women. There have been reports of liver cancer associated with long-term steroid use. In males there can be prostate gland troubles, shrinkage of the testicles, and a decrease in sperm production. Women can experience growth of hair in unusual places, enlargement of the clitoris, and menstrual troubles. These changes are not masked by the concurrent use of estrogens (female hormones), and in many cases are not reversible even when steroids are discontinued. Other side effects include nausea, loss of appetite, and increased or decreased sexual drive.

Another danger to steroids is an increase in tendon strength out of proportion with muscle strength. The tendons may become inflamed and rupture where the muscle and tendons join together.

There is also a behavioral effect associated with steroids. When athletes use them they think they train more aggressively and, in fact, many do. When they come off them, they feel depressed. Individual responses to different steroids vary widely, so athletes shop around and try different brands to see which are most effective for them.

An athlete who takes steroids is risking permanent medical complications and even death. That should be sufficient warning against them.

Steroids aren't the only substances showing up in drug tests. Athletes are also taking large amounts of caffeine, bicarbonate, bee pollen, and other substances to improve performance or delay fatigue. Though these substances are legal under UCI rules, some also have negative side effects.

Caffeine

For years cyclists have downed a small flask of strong coffee or coke syrup near the end of a race to get that last kick before the finish. Many cyclists also use caffeine before and during competition in the belief it will increase endurance.

In chemical terms, caffeine is Trimethylxanthine. It is found naturally in more than 60 plants, including coffee beans, tea leaves, kola nuts, and cocoa. The table shows the approximate amount of caffeine in various sources.

Caffeine, like amphetamine, stimulates the central nervous system. It has been found, like alcohol, to pass quickly through the bloodstream to the brain. Caffeine stimulates the kidneys and boosts the rate and depth of respiration and circulation. It dilates coronary arteries and increases the heart's force of contraction.

Caffeine also increases the body's capacity for muscular work by releasing stored fats into the system for energy, thus sparing carbohydrate stores for hard efforts during a race. A study in the late 1970s found that cyclists who ingested 330 milligrams of caffeine one hour before exercising at 80% of their maximum aerobic capacity were able to pedal 19.5% longer than those test subjects who did not use caffeine.

CAFFEINE IN VARIOUS PRODUCTS

BEVERAGES	Mg caffeine	STIMULANTS	
Brewed coffee	100-150/cup	No-Doz	100/tablet
Instant coffee	86-99/cup	Vivarine	200/tablet
Tea	60-75/cup		
Decaffeinated coffee	2-4/cup	ANALGESICS	
Cola drinks	40-60/glass	Anacin, Cope, Midol	32/tablet
COLD PREPARATIONS		Vanquish	60/tablet
Over-the-counter	30/tablet	Exerdrin	66/tablet

Caffeine is a stimulant that is allowed in competition but only within limits. It also poses many health hazards, depending on the individual and the amount ingested.

But there are hazards to caffeine use. It is addictive and your body will need ever-increasing amounts to achieve the same ergogenic effects. Caffeine is also a diuretic, stimulating urine flow. This fact, combined with the amount of liquid in several cups of coffee or tea, means you're likely to to need a pit stop during a race. In hot weather, the diuretic action can compound the serious problem of dehydration.

Many people also get upset stomachs when they drink large amounts of caffeine. Other adverse effects include restlessness, ringing in the ears, fast pulse, vomiting, fever, and tremors. In extreme cases, caffeine poisoning can even cause coma and death by cardiovascular and respiratory collapse.

Heavy use of caffeine may also lead to an increased risk of heart problems. Research indicates that consuming two to five cups of coffee or more per day may increase the risk of heart disease significantly. Caffeine has also been linked to high levels of cholesterol.

There are mixed opinions among cyclists and researchers over how much caffeine it takes to improve performance, as well as the best time to take it. For most road riders, drinking 1-2 cups of coffee 45-60 minutes before a race and periodically during the event seems to work well. Most riders see improvement when they take five mg of caffeine per kilogram of body weight. When riders take more more than seven mg per kilogram, they experience headaches and other side effects.

Caffeine use is currently allowed under International Olympic Committee rules but only within limits. In 1988 a U.S. cyclist lost his place on the Olympic team when urinalysis revealed caffeine levels slightly above the 12 micrograms per milliliter allowed under international rules.

Individual responses to caffeine vary widely, depending on the size of the rider, the intensity of the activity, and the differences in natural metabolism. If you drank six to eight cups of coffee in one sitting and were tested within two or three hours, you might test over the legal limit.

Soda loading

Sodium bicarbonate, more commonly known as baking soda, is growing in popularity as an ergogenic aid. It is taken before primarily anaerobic races to offset the build-up of lactic acid and thus delay fatigue.

On the negative side, bicarbonate may cause acute gastric distress and hypertension due to its high sodium content. Soda loading has also been known to cause diarrhea within one to three hours after ingestion.

Soda loading works by altering the acidity of the blood. Normally blood acidity is in the range of 7.35 to 7.45 on the pH scale, but it can drop to 7.0 during intense exercise. (The drop in pH indicates an increase in acidity.) Taking sodium bicarbonate has been shown to raise the pH so that lactic acid production is buffered and fatigue is delayed. More anaerobic work can be done before fatigue is reached. This works because bicarbonate speeds up the leakage of lactate from the muscle cells into the blood stream. Lactate in the cells is attracted to the greater concentration of bicarbonate in the blood.

A study of trained middle-distance runners showed that sodium bicarbonate improved performance. The test group took 300 mg of bicarbonate per kg of body weight prior to an 800-meter race. The result was significantly faster times, with five of the six subjects running an average of 2.9 seconds faster for the two-minute event.

Also in 1984, David Costill and his research team conducted a study that led to new findings about bicarbonate and its ability to delay the onset of fatigue. Rather than having subjects perform one bout of exercise for one to four minutes, as had been done in previous research, Costill had the cyclists do five one-minute bouts at 100% of max VO_2. The result was a significantly higher blood pH and muscle pH, allowing more energy to be produced anaerobically in subjects who used soda loading.

From this experiment researchers determined that sodium bicarbonate would be particularly beneficial in training. By using it, athletes may be able to train harder and longer before lactic acid accumulation causes fatigue and limits performance.

Although it is a performance enhancer, sodium bicarbonate is still a fair and legal substance that is not tested for by the International Olympic Committee. It is thought that it can be detected by measuring the pH of the urine, but currently the use of bicarbonate is not banned.

Blood boosting

In the never-ending search for greater oxygen delivery to working muscles, cyclists turned first to high-altitude training, then to blood boosting, which was used by several U.S. cyclists in the 1984 Olympic Games. Though the practice was declared illegal in 1985, I know of cyclists from several countries who blood boosted before the 1986 world cycling championships and are still doing so at major events. (One problem with controlling the practice is that it is extremely hard to detect.)

Here's how blood boosting works: 500-1,000 ml of blood are withdrawn from the athlete 3-4 weeks before competition and preserved by freezing. The athlete continues to train, and with the help of exercise and diet, the blood that was removed is regenerated. Then, just before competition, he is reinfused with his own blood. This gives him an abundance of oxygen-carrying red blood cells, which theoretically should improve performance.

Research conducted with highly trained endurance runners found that, in fact, blood boosting increased hemoglobin concentration by 8% and oxygen consumption by 4 ml/kg. The researchers concluded that blood boosting does increase max VO_2 and extend endurance. The advantages last up to one week after reinfusion.

But there are big drawbacks. Blood boosting can increase the viscosity, or thickness, of the blood, which can lead to clotting in blood vessels and possible heart failure. The transfusion itself can lead to infection of the liver. If another person's blood is used, the possibility of contracting AIDS also exists.

Blood boosting is currently banned under IOC and USCF rules.

Erythropoietin

Erythropoietin, or EPO, is a substance with an effect similar to blood boosting. Produced by the kidneys, EPO is a hormone that stimulates and controls the production of red blood cells. Recent advances in genetic engineering have also made it possible to produce synthetic EPO.

Because EPO stimulates red blood cell production, some athletes have apparently been using it for competitive gain. EPO appears to increase endurance just as blood boosting does, and it acts more quickly, reliably, and potently. After EPO is injected it clears the body in about 24 hours. but it can stimulate red blood cell production for up to 14 days. EPO also is undetectable by current tests.

But using EPO is dangerous, especially to endurance cyclists. Like blood boosting, it can increase blood viscosity, which in turn can lead to cerebral or cardiovascular ischemia and vascular clotting. In simple terms, the thickened blood begins to move to the vital organs more slowly. It also clots more quickly, increasing the chances of heart attack and stroke

Several young European cyclists have died of heart problems in the recent past. Had they been experimenting with EPO? No one is sure, but the recent inexplicably high incidence of death and heart disease among riders has prompted at least one European government to begin an investigation.

EPO was added to the banned list in the late 1980's. While there is no specific test to measure exogenous levels of EPO, the UCI is measuring hematocrit (the percentage of red blood cells in the blood) to help determine if a cyclist's blood has become too concentrated.

Ephedrine

Ephedrine is an ingredient in many prescription and over-the-counter medications used to treat respiratory ailments. It is on the IOC list of banned substances because some scientists and physicians think it stimulates work output.

Ephedrine is believed to affect the sympathetic nervous system, which controls changes in heart rate and cardiac output and regulates the release of adrenaline. No favorable effect on athletic performance has ever been conclusively demonstrated with the use of ephedrine.

However, because both ephedrine and pseudoephedrine are widely used in oral and spray products, a cyclist who innocently takes a cold medication can end up testing positive. Such a situation occurred a few years ago at the Coors Classic stage race when a national-class woman rider took half an adult dose of Nyquil for relief of cold symptoms. She tested positive the next day, was disqualified from the event, and suspended from racing.

The way things stand now, any trace of a banned substance in the urine is considered doping. New regulations are needed to make a distinction between medical levels and ergogenic levels.

Oxygen

Many cyclists use oxygen as an ergogenic aid. I've known riders who inhaled it before several stages in the high-altitude Coors Classic in Colorado, and others who experimented with it at the national track championships as an aid to recovery.

Some cyclists and researchers believe that increasing the oxygen content of inhaled air may be a way to improve oxygen use in the body. In fact, breathing extra oxygen during exercise has been shown to improve performance. The exercise can be performed with lower heart rates, lower breathing rates, and lower lactic acid levels. But there are few situations where oxygen can be used during competition, unless you want to replace a water bottle with an oxygen tank.

Is it beneficial to breathe extra oxygen before exercising? Recent studies conducted with swimmers showed no improvement in performance when oxygen was inhaled 4-5 minutes before a 100-yard freestyle swim. Several other studies failed to find any benefit to using oxygen if the exercise lasted longer than two minutes. However, in one study, subjects breathed oxygen before, during, and after a submaximal treadmill run, which resulted in lower pulse rates at rest and during the first few minutes of exercise.

So it appears that breathing oxygen before competition may have some beneficial effect, though it is limited. The time between oxygen breathing and the beginning of competition can be no longer than two minutes and the helpful effects will not last much longer than two minutes.

Does oxygen aid recovery? So far, very few studies have been done on oxygen use after exercise. But according to the results now in, the benefit to later performance is small and probably inconsequential. Since in most cycling programs there is ample time for recovery between events, oxygen as an aid to recovery may be of little use.

Bee pollen

One of the more unlikely ergogenic aids is bee pollen, which enjoyed a heyday in the late '70s and early '80s. The sellers of pollen claim their product will give you greater energy, stamina, and strength. It is, they say, the miracle energy booster for fatigued muscles.

Sound too good to be true? Well, it probably is. All the controlled studies published in scientific journals show that bee pollen does not improve athletic performance. One study evaluated the training effect of taking 400 mg of bee pollen versus a placebo (400 mg of brown sugar) every day for 75 days. The 46 subjects were tested for strength and endurance before and after the experiment. The pollen takers exhibited no greater improvement in fitness or performance.

In another study, swimmers at Louisiana State University participated in a 6-month experiment in which half the team took 10 pollen tablets a day, one-quarter received 10 placebo tablets each day, and the other one-quarter received 5 pollen and 5 placebos. There was no measurable difference in performance between the three groups.

The research clearly shows that many nutritional claims about bee pollen do not stand up to valid scientific study.

In addition, taking pollen can be dangerous, prompting a severe allergic reaction in 10-20% of the population. Some pollen is collected from sunflowers, ragweed, or dandelions and may cause reactions in people who are sensitive to those substances. In one instance, an individual with a history of seasonal allergy went into shock within 15 minutes of taking bee pollen and required emergency treatment.

Appendix 1
Recognizing and Dealing with Overtraining

Physical and Psychological Characteristics of Staleness

<u>Physical Changes</u>

Muscle soreness

Gradual weight loss

Athlete looks drawn

Swelling of lymph nodes

Increase morning heart rate

Heavy leggedness

Constipation or diarrhea

Inability to complete training

Fatigue

Flu-like symptoms

Emotional and Behavioral Changes

Irritability

Loss of enthusiasm

Lack of appetite

Depression

Anxiety

Easily irritated

Desire to quit training

Sleep disturbances

Loss of self-confidence

Inability to concentrate

Preventing Overtraining

What can be done to prevent this ailment before it begins to occur? You can take the following measures into account to prevent overtraining from occurring:

1. Sleep at least eight hours at night when hard training is being conducted.

2. Eat a balanced diet that includes all the basic nutrients.

3. Conduct at least 8 to 10 weeks of endurance work to build up a good base of conditioning. Do not increase the frequency, duration and intensity of the training sessions too quickly.

4. Gradually build up the quantity and quality of training, so that you are prepared both physically and mentally for the volume of training and competition.

5. Many coaches recommend a 15–30 minute nap before the afternoon workout.

6. When hard training is being conducted, the intensity of the training should be individualized to your level of fitness and experience.

7. Know yourself and how you react to training stress and continually review your training logs to monitor stress and training goals.

8. Use a training diary and record morning pulse rate, body weight, sleep patterns, medical and training problems and record all your training sessions on a daily basis.

9. Rest is also an important component of training. Use rest days on a periodic basis to make you stronger.

Appendix 2
Scientific definitions for cyclists

Adenosine triphosphate (ATP) — a compound formed from the breakdown of food and stored in all cells, especially muscle. When it is split by enzyme action, energy is produced. ATP is believed to be the last chemical formed just before the transfer of chemical work to mechanical work.

aerobic exercise — (literally, exercise "with oxygen") an intensity of exercise below the level which produces lactic acid faster than the muscle cells can dispose of it. Energy needs are met by oxygen breathed in and thus no oxygen debt is incurred. Such exercise can be continued for long periods.

alactacid oxygen debt — the oxygen necessary after strenuous exercise to replenish the ATP-PC energy stores.

amino acids — the structural components of protein. There are 20 amino acids, of which 11 are termed essential, meaning they are not produced in the body and must be obtained through food.

amphetamine — a synthetic central nervous system stimulant related to epinephrine (adrenaline).

anabolic steroids — a group of synthetic drugs that have an anabolic (protein building) effect on the body. Though used by some athletes to gain muscular strength, steroids are considered dangerous because of their side effects and are illegal in competition.

anaerobic exercise — (literally, exercise "without oxygen") exercise that demands more oxygen than the heart and lungs can supply. Thus, an oxygen debt occurs during the short period the exercise intensity can be maintained.

ATP-PC system — an anaerobic energy system in which ATP is formed from the breakdown of phosphocreatine (PC). Muscles performing at maximal effort for 10 seconds or less obtain ATP from this system.

blood pressure — the pressure exerted by the blood on the wall of the blood vessel. It varies with age, sex, altitude, muscular development, fatigue, mental stress, etc.

calorie — a measure of heat energy; the amount of heat needed to raise one gram of water one degree Celsius. A Calorie (upper case C) is 1,000 calories and is also called a kilocalorie (abbreviated kcal).

carbohydrate — an organic compound containing only carbon, hydrogen, and oxygen molecules. It is a basic source of energy, being stored as glycogen in most body tissues but principally in the liver and muscles. Sources of carbohydrates include whole grains, vegetables, potatoes, fruits, honey, and refined sugars. Carbohydrates provide about four calories per gram.

cardiac output — the amount of blood pumped by the heart per minute. At rest, about six to eight liters per minute in adults.

complete protein — protein that contains all the essential amino acids. Some foods that contain complete proteins are cheese, eggs, milk, and meat.

electrolytes — ionized salts in blood, tissue fluids, and cells.

energy — the capacity for doing work.

enzymes — complex proteins that are capable of speeding up chemical changes in other substances without being changed themselves. Enzymes are present in digestive juices, where they cause food to break down into simpler compounds.

ergogenic aids — substances or devices used to improve athletic performance.

ergometer — a stationary bicycle used for training or for laboratory tests to measure work performed.

fast-twitch (FT) muscle fibers — fibers with a contraction speed two to three times faster than slow-twitch (ST) fibers. Fast-twitch fibers are characterized by fast contraction time, high anaerobic capacity, and low aerobic capacity. They are capable of producing more power than ST fibers.

fat — a soft tissue in the body. Fat supplies a concentrated source of fuel, storage of energy and certain vitamins, insulation, and support and protection of organs. Fat stores are metabolized when blood sugar is below normal. A gram of fat has nine calories.

glucose (blood sugar) — the most important carbohydrate in body metabolism. In the tissue it may be converted into glycogen, used to form fat, or oxidized to carbon dioxide and water.

glycogen — the form in which carbohydrates are stored in the body. When needed, it is converted by the tissues into glucose. It is used by muscles and, with their contraction, breaks down into lactic acid. Oxygen is then needed to convert lactic acid back to glycogen, at which time some of the lactic acid is burned.

glycolysis — the enzymatic breakdown of glucose to produce ATP.

hemoglobin — the iron-containing pigment that enables red blood cells to carry oxygen from the lungs to the tissues.

hyperventilation — an excessive increase in the rate of breathing, which causes a decrease in the amount of carbon dioxide in the blood. The result can be giddiness, cramps, convulsions, lowered blood pressure, and anxiety. The treatment is to breathe into a paper bag or close one nostril and breath with the mouth shut, thereby helping the blood's carbon dioxide content return to normal.

incomplete protein — protein that lacks one or more of the essential amino acids. Examples of foods with incomplete proteins are grains and vegetables.

interval training — a system in which short periods of hard exercise are interspersed with easier exercise for recovery.

isokinetic exercise — contraction of a muscle during which the force is exerted while the muscle shortening is maximal.

isometric exercise — contraction of a muscle in which shortening or lengthening is prevented. Tension is developed but no mechanical work is performed.

isotonic exercise — contraction of a muscle during which the force of resistance to the movement remains constant throughout the range of motion.

lactacid oxygen debt — the oxygen necessary after strenuous exercise to remove lactic acid from the blood.

lactic acid — a chemical compound formed in exercising muscles by the breakdown of glycogen (glycolsis). It causes the immediate muscular pain associated with severe exercise.

maximal oxygen consumption (max VO_2) — the maximum amount of oxygen that an individual can take in in one minute. The figure may be expressed in liters of oxygen per minute (l/min) or, more commonly, milliliters of oxygen per kilogram of body weight per minute (ml/kg/min).

minerals — inorganic elements or compounds that are essential constituents of all cells. Minerals play an important role in water metabolism, regulation of blood volume, and maintenance of proper acid-base balance. They regulate the sensitivity of muscle and nerve tissue to stimulation. Mineral salts are excreted daily and must be replaced through diet.

myoglobin — a protein within muscle tissue responsible for oxygen transport and storage.

oxygen debt — the amount of oxygen required after muscular activity for the removal of lactic acid and other metabolic products that accumulate when the supply of oxygen is below the needs of the individual.

oxygen deficit — the time during exercise in which the level of oxygen consumption does not equal what is necessary to supply all the ATP. Energy is partially supplied from anaerobic stores.

pH — the degree of acidity or alkalinity of a substance. Neutral is pH 7. Increasing acidity is expressed as a number less than 7; increasing alkalinity is expressed as a number greater than 7. The normal pH of blood plasma is 7.35-7.45.

power — the rate at which work is done. For example, if 1 pound is raised 10 feet in 1 minute, power is expressed as 10 foot-pounds per minute.

protein — a food substance formed from amino acids. Proteins are essential for growth, for building new tissue, and for repairing injured or broken-down tissue. Good sources are milk, eggs, cheese, meat, fish, and some vegetables such as soy beans. One gram of protein supplies four calories.

pyruvate — pyruvic acid, the final product in aerobic exercise.

slow-twitch (ST) muscle fibers — fibers that contract at a rate two to three times slower than fast-twitch (FT) fibers. Slow-twitch fibers are characterized by slow contraction time, low anaerobic capacity, and high aerobic capacity and are associated with great endurance.

strength — the force that a muscle can exert in one maximal effort.

ventilation — the movement of air in and out of the lungs, resulting in the oxygenation of blood.

vital capacity — the greatest volume of air that can be expelled following the deepest possible inspiration.

vitamins — complex organic substances indispensable for normal body functions and health maintenance. Vitamins act chiefly as regulators of metabolic processes and play a role in energy transformations. However, they are not sources of energy.

work — application of force through distance. For example, moving five pounds a distance of one foot equals five foot-pounds of work.

Index

Other Books from Vitesse Press

Bicycle Road Racing by Edward Borysewicz $24.95
A complete road-racing program by former National Coach Eddie B.

Road Racing: Technique & Training by Bernard Hinault $17.95
Racing and training tips from a five-time Tour de France winner.

Massage For Cyclists by Roger Pozeznik $14.95
Clear advice and excellent photos of massage sequences. 2nd Printing.

Mountain Biking For Women by Robin Stuart & Cathy Jensen $15.00
Woman to woman advice and instruction from two experienced cyclists.

Central New York Mountain Biking by Dick Mansfield $12.95
Thirty of the best back road and trail rides in upstate New York.

Vermont Mountain Biking by Dick Mansfield $10.95
Twenty-four rides in southern Vermont.

Fit and Pregnant by Joan Butler $16.00
Advice from a nurse-midwife who is an athlete and mother. Fourth printing.

Runner's Guide To Cross Country Skiing by Dick Mansfield $10.95
Still the best source for runners looking for a winter alternative.

Canoe Racing by Peter Heed $14.95
The "bible" of flat water canoe racing. Third printing.

We encourage you to buy our books at a bookstore or sports shop. When ordering directly from Vitesse, prepayment or a credit card number and expiration date is required. Please include the price of the book plus handling ($2.50 for the first book, $1.00 for each additional book) and 5% sales tax for Maryland addresses.

Telephone 301-772-5915   Fax 301-772-5921

Postal Orders: VITESSE PRESS, 4431 Lehigh Road, #288, College Park, MD 20740

Email: dickmfield@aol.com   Web site: www.acornpub.com